MEDIEVAL NOTARIES AND THEIR ACTS
The 1327–1328 Register of Jean Holanie

Documents of Practice Series

This series, published by Medieval Institute Publications at Western Michigan University in conjunction with TEAMS, is designed to offer a focused collection of primary-source materials in a classroom-friendly format. Though the topics illuminated by these booklets are generally familiar to teachers and students in various fields of medieval studies, the booklets allow readers to concentrate on a single topic or theme, either as the principal reading for a specific unit or topic within a course or as a running supplement to topics and readings being used through a semester. The topics have been chosen so they either can be seen as focal points of attention on their own, or can be used to offer a historical dimension to material used in courses on literature, women's studies, the history of medicine, religious studies, and other such areas—areas that draw a wide range of students who are being introduced to the use of primary materials and to interdisciplinary and many-layered views of the structure of medieval society and culture.

General Editor of the Series
Joel T. Rosenthal, *State University of New York–Stony Brook*

Advisory Editorial Board
Charlotte Newman Goldy, *Miami University of Ohio*
William Chester Jordan, *Princeton University*
Ralph V. Turner, *Florida State University (Emeritus)*

MEDIEVAL NOTARIES AND THEIR ACTS
The 1327–1328 Register of Jean Holanie

Introduced, Edited, and Translated by
Kathryn L. Reyerson
and
Debra A. Salata

Published for TEAMS
(The Consortium for the Teaching of the Middle Ages)

by

MEDIEVAL INSTITUTE PUBLICATIONS
Kalamazoo, Michigan
2004

Printed in the United States of America
P   6   5   4   3   2

Cover and design by Linda K. Judy

Composed by Julie Scrivener

ISBN 1-58044-081-9

Library of Congress Cataloging-in-Publication Data

Medieval notaries and their acts : the 1327-1328 register of Jean
Holanie / introduced, edited, and translated by Kathryn L. Reyerson and
Debra A. Salata.
    p. cm. -- (Documents of practice series)
    ISBN 1-58044-081-9 (pbk. : alk. paper)
    1. Notaries--France--Montpellier--History--To 1500--Sources. 2. Law,
Medieval--Sources. 3. Holanie, Jean. I. Holanie, Jean. II. Reyerson,
Kathryn. III. Salata, Debra A., 1953- IV. Series.
    KJV254.M43 2004
    347.44'016--dc22
                                                        2003026034

CONTENTS

ACKNOWLEDGMENTS

We are indebted to Marguerite Ragnow, Associate Director of the Center for Early Modern History at the University of Minnesota, for her editorial suggestions. Thanks are also due generations of graduate students in Kathryn Reyerson's seminars at the University of Minnesota who participated in the transcription of the Holanie register and in the analysis of documents, especially Clifford Backman, Susan Duxbury, and Elizabeth Dachowski. Any remaining errors are the editors' alone.

We wish to thank the Archives Départementales de l'Hérault for permission to reproduce the first folio of the Holanie register as an illustration. We are grateful to Martine Sainte-Marie, archiviste-paléographe, for her assistance over the years in the notarial archives of Montpellier. Kathryn Reyerson would like to acknowledge support from the Graduate School of the University of Minnesota for multiple Grants-in-Aid for RAships over many years in connection with this project.

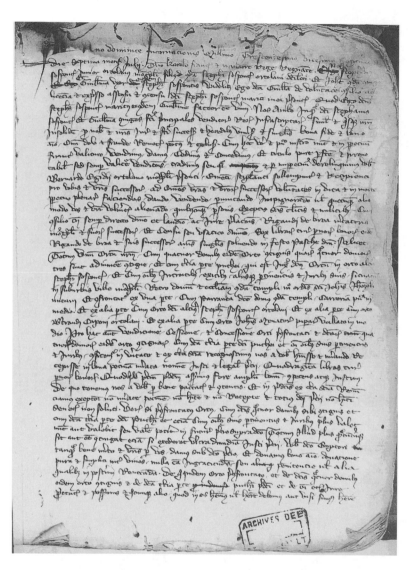

Plate 1. First folio of the Holanie register. Archives Départmentales de l'Hérault.

INTRODUCTION

THE NOTARIAL FUNCTION IN
THE MEDIEVAL EUROPEAN CONTEXT

Southern Europe enjoyed an extensive notarial culture in the Middle Ages. As public scribes, notaries were responsible for writing down legal documents for public officials and private persons who requested and paid for their services. Notaries recorded a variety of contracts relating to business arrangements, trade, finance, family, marriage, inheritance, and real estate. They were appointed by various political powers: kings, nobles, popes, bishops, emperors, municipal governments, and other public authorities. These political authorities often had their own notaries who recorded official acts. Private persons were free to hire the notary of their choice. Notaries could testify in a court of law to the legal authenticity of the documents they wrote even without any of the parties to the contracts being present. Theoretically, the notarial contract itself constituted legal proof of the agreement. Thus, notaries played an important legal role in the activities of everyday life.

The beginnings of the continental European notarial tradition are explored in this short book, which will acquaint readers with the format of notarial documents, with registers (the books containing notarial acts), and with the variety of notarial acts. Recordkeeping had become essential in the complex economic world of commerce and finance. The notary emerged as a notetaker, precision recordkeeper, stationer, repository of legal representation, and facilitator of the exchange of information. Increased literacy was required among members of the merchant

1

classes, who had some schooling, resulting in their greater use of written documents in financial transactions and in long-distance trade. Literacy, in turn, was a significant impetus in the development of trade in Western Europe. The notary was an ally of urban and rural inhabitants, framing in legal documents their obligations of new operations in commerce and finance and more traditional real estate transactions which had often historically taken written form.

Sample documents of this book have been selected for their internal content and interest and for their illustration of specific types of contracts. These acts have been drawn from a single notarial register of 1327–28, written by the royal public notary, Jean Holanie, of the southern French town of Montpellier. In the fourteenth century, Montpellier was a thriving urban center with a population of upwards of 40,000 inhabitants, located about ten kilometers from the Mediterranean. Commerce and finance dominated the business life of Montpellier, bringing foreign merchants to town. A university of law, medicine, and the arts drew students from all over Europe.

HISTORICAL DEVELOPMENT

Italy and other Mediterranean countries share with southern France a common notarial tradition based on a written Roman legal heritage. The office of notary developed out of the classical Roman offices of *notarius, tabellio,* and *tabularius* (see Glossary for unfamiliar terms), whose holders' main responsibility was to prepare legal documents for the Roman government.[1] Justinian's *Digest* and *Code* (sixth century C.E.) described the Roman office of notary. The *notarius* recorded the dictation of private parties and governmental officials in notebooks. The *tabellio* then drew up the official documents from the notes of the *notarius*. The *tabularius* recorded obligations of debt due the Roman Treasury and foreshadowed the medieval money changer as well as the notary. The offices and duties of the Roman *notarius, tabellio,* and *tabularius* were merged into the medieval office of the notary by the eleventh

---

[1]James Cowie Brown, *The Origin and Early History of the Office of Notary* (Edinburgh: W. Green & Son, 1936), 9–21.

and twelfth centuries which was when the notary can again be documented in western Europe.

While there is evidence of offices with scribal responsibilities earlier, the notarial practice associated with medieval Europe can be traced to the late eleventh century in Italy with the revival of Roman law study at the University of Bologna.[2] Over the course of the twelfth century, notarial usage spread throughout those areas of Europe which were influenced by the revival of Roman law, particularly Italy and southern France. Beyond Roman law, factors such as the growth of bureaucratic institutions of government, the growing complexities of international trade, and innovations in business practice contributed to the need for written documents. Southern Europe, especially Italy, was in the forefront of commercial revival and innovation, beginning in the eleventh century.

Southern France enjoyed early and frequent contacts with Italian towns, the pacesetters in legal and institutional developments in western Europe in the eleventh and twelfth centuries. The revival of Roman law and the emergence of municipal government institutions (consulates) in southern French towns in the first half of the twelfth century followed similar developments in Italy by approximately half a century. With the growth of court systems and government based upon a written-law tradition, the documentary records took various forms; notarial registers, municipal statutes, chronicles, and charters complemented seigneurial and episcopal cartulary notices.[3]

In their heyday, medieval Italian towns could count hundreds of practicing notaries. In the late thirteenth century there were over two hundred notaries exercising their function in Pisa; two hundred working in Genoa in 1303; six hundred in Florence in 1336–38, according to the Florentine chronicler and businessman, Giovanni Villani; and fifteen hundred in Milan in 1288, according to the Milanese writer,

---

[2]See David Herlihy, "The Notarial Chartulary," in *Pisa in the Early Renaissance. A Study of Urban Growth* (New Haven: Yale University Press, 1958), 1–20.

[3]The bibliographic essay, "Suggestions for Further Reading," provides examples of edited notarial registers.

Bonvesin della Riva.[4] In fourteenth-century Montpellier the names of as many as seventy notaries can be noted in a single year, and there were probably significantly more in practice. These numbers alone suggest the tremendous impact of notarial culture on medieval Europe.[5]

NOTARIES IN NORTHERN EUROPE

Notaries in northern Europe did not follow the Roman notarial model as they did in southern Europe, where notaries were trained in Roman law; licensed by a public authority such as a municipality, bishop, king, or emperor; registered their documents as public records; and, when necessary, authenticated their documents in courts of law. Instead, northern notaries served primarily as bureaucratic scribes, administrators, or secretaries to various ecclesiastical and lay officials. Charlemagne (768–814) had resurrected the office of notary. In Carolingian Europe notaries served both as scribes for bishops, counts, and dukes, and as administrators in charge of collecting revenues.[6] Although the administrative role of notaries can be found in the time of Charles the Good, Count of Flanders (1119–27), the scribal role of notaries was the one that prevailed throughout northern Europe. In twelfth-century England, John of Salisbury dictated letters to his notary who served as his secretary.[7] In a similar fashion in twelfth-century Saxony, notaries issued legal

---

[4]R. S. Lopez, "The Unexplored Wealth of the Notarial Archives of Pisa and Lucca," *Mélanges d'histoire du moyen âge dédiés à la mémoire de Louis Halphen* (Paris: Presses Universitaires de France, 1951), 417–32; Herlihy, *Pisa in the Early Renaissance*, 1–10. On the statistics of Bonvesin della Riva and Giovanni Villani, see Robert S. Lopez and Irving W. Raymond, *Medieval Trade in the Mediterranean World. Illustrative Documents Translated with Introductions and Notes* (New York: Columbia University Press, 1955, 1961), 65 and 72.

[5]For a discussion of notarial culture, see Kathryn Reyerson, *The Art of the Deal: Intermediaries of Trade in Medieval Montpellier*, The Medieval Mediterranean 37 (Leiden: E. J. Brill, 2002).

[6]James M. Murray, *Notarial Instruments in Flanders between 1280 and 1452* (Brussels: Commission Royale d'Histoire/Koninklijke Commissie voor Geschiedenis, 1995), 4.

[7]M. T. Clanchy, *From Memory to Written Record. England 1066–1307* (Oxford, U.K., and Cambridge, Mass.: Blackwell, 1979, 1993), 126.

documents and recorded legal transactions for the chancery of Henry the Lion, Duke of Bavaria and Saxony (1139–95).[8] Holy Roman Emperor Frederick II (1215–50) promulgated a peace statute in 1235 which provided that all justiciars have notaries to record writs, judicial proceedings, judgments issued, and all documents regarding outlaws.[9] King Philip IV of France (1285–1314) even created a department of royal notaries to record official documents.[10]

While notarial practice existed in northern Europe in the Middle Ages, the use of public notaries for private recordkeeping remained a southern European phenomenon. During the thirteenth century, the role of northern notaries gradually changed from private scribes and administrators to one more closely approximating the role of public notaries in southern Europe. Some political authorities began requiring notaries to be trained and licensed in order to authenticate documents. The Emperor required licensed notaries to pass an examination and take an oath of office similar to the procedure required of the notaries licensed by papal authority.[11] Notarial practice in England, however, never conformed to the Roman model as it did in the rest of Europe; this insular deviation is attributed to the development of common law and the relatively slight influence that Roman law had in England.[12] English notaries continued to serve bureaucratic functions, but their role and training were neither uniform nor regulated. The Statute of Merchants in 1285 attempted to standardize the recording of commercial documents, but clerks, rather than notaries, continued to record these documents.[13] Even though English notaries played a less important legal

[8]Harold J. Berman, *Law and Revolution. The Formation of the Western Legal Tradition* (Cambridge, Mass.: Harvard University Press, 1983), 507–08.

[9]Berman, *Law and Revolution*, 501.

[10]Murray, *Notarial Instruments in Flanders*, 13.

[11]Murray, *Notarial Instruments in Flanders*, 7.

[12]The office of notary developed rather late in England. Clanchy, in his book, *From Memory to Written Record*, describes the process by which England began to use written documents and thus needed scribes and notaries. Clanchy, 298, argues that the office of notary did not develop sooner in England because English law was based upon customary law rather than a Roman law model.

[13]Clanchy, *From Memory to Written Record*, 307–08.

role in recording and authenticating commercial transactions, municipal and guild clerks recorded and certified such transactions so that they could be admitted as legal evidence in English courts of law.

Notarial traditions, similar though not identical to those of southern Europe, appeared in the North in the late thirteenth century.[14] In part, this was due to Italian influence and a merchant diaspora. Italian merchants, trading in the Low Countries and in northern France, brought their own practices with them.[15] Thus one finds notaries responsible for recording and authenticating legal documents in the North after 1300.

SURVIVAL OF NOTARIAL REGISTERS

The survival rates of notarial registers in southern Europe are understandably highest in Italy, given Italy's position in the forefront of economic development in the Middle Ages. The earliest extant register is that of Giovanni Scriba (1154–66) of the Italian town of Genoa. Other registers of Genoa have survived from the late twelfth century, and some two hundred have survived from the thirteenth century. The rates of survival for Genoa increase dramatically from that point on, with thousands of registers from the fourteenth century. Other Italian towns, such as Lucca and Pisa, preserve registers from the thirteenth century. It is fair to say that wherever Italian merchants traveled, their notaries accompanied them. Thus, there are survivals of registers from the Near East, from Pera, a suburb of Constantinople that was the site of a Genoese colony, and from Caffa in the Black Sea area where the Genoese also had a colony. Northern Europe has surviving registers of Italian notaries of the late thirteenth–fourteenth centuries in Bruges, Ghent, and Ypres, recording the business of foreign merchants, particularly Italians.[16]

---

[14]Murray, *Notarial Instruments in Flanders*, 12–15.

[15]Raymond de Roover, *Money, Banking and Credit in Mediaeval Bruges: Italian Merchant-Bankers, Lombards and Money-Changers* (Cambridge, Mass.: Harvard University Press, 1948).

[16]James M. Murray, "Failure of corporation: Notaries public in medieval Bruges," *Journal of Medieval History* 12 (1986): 155–66; and de Roover, *Money,*

Overall, southern France—the provinces of Provence and Langue-doc—and Spain preserve many fewer notarial registers than Italy. Registers survive in Roussillon, Majorca, and the Iberian Peninsula, beginning in the late thirteenth century. Seventeen registers of the thirteenth century remain at Perpignan, while several hundred are preserved there from the fourteenth century, and Spanish archives also contain a wealth of fourteenth-century survivals.[17] Provence has some extant thirteenth-century registers and many more from the fourteenth in towns such as Marseille and Manosque.[18] For the period 1350–1450 there are two hundred registers remaining from Toulouse in Upper Languedoc.

The profession of public notary, first termed *tabellio*, can be found in the Lower Languedocian town of Montpellier in the mid-twelfth century at a time when Roman legal terminology was becoming increasingly common in local sources.[19] The earliest and only thirteenth-century register preserved in Montpellier is that of Jean Grimaud (1293–94).[20] Jean Holanie wrote the register from which sample documents

Banking and Credit. By the sixteenth century one finds notarial registers for northern France as well as southern France, opening up vast resources for exploitation by historians. For example, there has been work done recently on the notarial registers of Ancien Régime Paris by Philip Hoffman, Gilles Postel-Vinay, and Jean-Laurent Rosenthal, "Information and Economic History: How the Credit Market in Old Régime Paris Forces Us to Rethink the Transition to Capitalism," *American Historical Review* 104 (1999): 69–94.

[17]Various archives in Barcelona and in Valencia preserve notarial registers termed *protocolos*.

[18]About thirty registers survive in Marseille for the thirteenth century, a comparable number at Manosque, one from Grasse and one from Cabasse.

[19]In the second half of the twelfth century, notaries appeared in the service of the Guilhem family, lords of Montpellier, and in the early thirteenth century in the employ of the new municipal government of twelve consuls to whom the new lord of Montpellier, Peter II of Aragon, along with his wife Marie, heiress of Montpellier, granted semi-autonomous status in a charter of 1204.

[20]Archives Municipales de Montpellier (hereafter abbreviated as A. M. Montpellier), II 1, Jean Grimaud: 1293–94. Holanie's register is the first in the series of registers preserved in the Archives Départementales de l'Hérault in the *fonds* (collection) entitled "notaires de l'évêché." These particular records are still in the process of being classified, though there exists a manuscript inventory in the archives. The registers of the municipal archives have been inventoried for the years 1293–1387. Aside from a grouping of acts associated

in this book have been chosen in 1327–28. Over the years 1293–1348 thirteen registers in all are preserved in the municipal and departmental archives of Montpellier.[21] With a hiatus from 1348 to the early 1360s, due in all likelihood to visitations of the Black Plague, extant registers for the second half of the fourteenth century number about fifty, with many more surviving in the fifteenth century.

Though not as numerous as Italian registers, those of southern France and Spain are equally valuable sources for the historian. The extant registers furnish information regarding the social, economic, juridical, financial, even religious activities of the inhabitants of the towns as well as of foreigners visiting the towns in which the acts were written. However, as historical evidence, notarial acts must be used with care. The survival rates of notarial registers vary from town to town, but in all cases in every locale, there were losses due to wars, fires, and random destruction. Of the remaining registers some, though not all, appear to survive intact, as they were written. Thus, the record is incomplete, and the evidence notarial acts provide is not all-inclusive. Notarial registers do not offer the quantitative possibilities of fiscal inventories. They can be useful for the elucidation of economic techniques and structures, but they are not reliable for the development of statistics or quantitative studies. The problems of only partial survival of all the notarial acts once written can be overcome, to a degree, by a consideration of the representativeness of the surviving registers.

---

with the notary Simon de Corneforti, there are only two registers older than the Holanie register of 1327–28, preserved in the Montpellier municipal archives and drafted by the notary Jean Grimaud, 1293–94 and 1301–02. There are five registers in all from the pen of Jean Holanie, additional registers having been preserved for 1333, 1336, 1342, and 1343–44, the latter being a collaborative effort with other notaries, coming perhaps at the end of Holanie's career (Archives Départementales de l'Hérault, hereafter abbreviated A. D. Hérault, II E 95/368–372, J. Holanie).

[21]Notarial archives were kept by various political authorities, both secular and ecclesiastical. In many cases notarial ateliers or workshops preserved registers over generations of notaries and centuries of existence. Modern archivists in France are still entering notarial registers into their archival collections and at times encounter a register from the Middle Ages, though this is less common today than in the early twentieth century.

People of medieval southern Europe went to the notary much more often than do modern Americans.[22] Notarial contracts allow the historian to delve into levels of society not easily reached by royal and noble records. The breadth of participation in notarial contracts of the urban and village population of southern Europe permits a detailed view of the economic and social strategies of individual families and of social and occupational groups. The notarial clientele presents multiple identities within the urban setting or village population.[23]

Notarial source materials for the Middle Ages remain largely unpublished in the archives of the Mediterranean world and in a broader geography for the Early Modern Era. If they appear in print, it is often in the form of synopses of acts. While there have been many monographs written by historians of economy, society, and law using notarial evidence, these sources still have many secrets to divulge to the next generations of medieval historians.

SOCIAL POSITION AND TRAINING OF THE MEDIEVAL NOTARY

As members of a paralegal profession in southern Europe, where written legal tradition and business practice necessitated frequent record-keeping, the economic and social status enjoyed by the notary was undoubtedly high, just behind that of lawyers and judges. Notaries played an important legal role in the economy and, indeed, in everyday life. Notarial ethics were supervised by licensing political authorities. In fact, royal and municipal statutory regulations for medieval notaries required them to be laymen of good reputation, as well as long-term residents of the locale where they practiced. Men, not women, were admitted to the notariate. An age requirement of thirty and a residency requirement of ten years existed for Montpellier notaries.[24] A schedule of fees, depending

---

[22]See Note on Modern Notaries, below.

[23]See Kathryn Reyerson and John Drendel, eds., *Urban and Rural Communities in Medieval France, Provence and Languedoc, 1000–1500* (Leiden: E. J. Brill, 1998) for articles treating the notariate in town and village.

[24]*Le Petit Thalamus de Montpellier*, ed. F. Pégat et al. (Montpellier, 1840), 120–24, in a statute of Jacme I the Conqueror, king of Aragon and lord of Montpellier, issued 17 August 1231.

on the type of instrument being executed, accompanied this statute. Simple debt contracts cost 4 *d.* while guardianships cost 18 *d.*, and contracts for house rentals 8 *d.*[25] In the fourteenth century actual rental costs for prestigious houses in Montpellier might be as high as 40 *l.* a year; thus the contract arranging the rental represented a tiny fraction of the size of the transaction itself.[26] Notaries were frequently mandated to have paralegal instruction at the university level. No statutory regulations remain concerning notarial instruction or apprenticeship at Montpellier, but municipal statutes specifying notarial training have survived at Marseille, Tarascon, and elsewhere in the south of France, as well as in Italy.

Stretching across the whole of the European coast of the western Mediterranean basin, there existed a consistent notarial culture of which merchants and other travelers could avail themselves. Notaries were literate in one or more of the vernacular languages spoken by their clients, including the various French, Italian, and Spanish dialects, and in notarial Latin, with a rote knowledge, if not complete understanding, of legal formulas such as those used to guarantee contracts and to assure exemptions from legal prosecution. Notaries had to interpret the legal technicalities of the contracts for their clients who were not necessarily literate and who, in all likelihood, did not understand Latin. Because of their exposure to legal and business worlds, notaries needed to be well versed in practical know-how of various kinds.

At odds with the respected status of notaries was their depiction in contemporary literature. Dante (1265–1321), Boccaccio (1313–75), and Chaucer (1340–1400) all portrayed the medieval notary, invariably in a very negative light. Dante, speaking of the Florentine notary Brunetto Latini (ca. 1210–94), acknowledged that clerks were "Men notable in letters, high in fame, / Who yet on earth bore one sin's bestial marks."[27]

---

[25]The reference is to pennies of Melgorian coinage. See Glossary.

[26]The quotation is in Tournois coinage. See Glossary. Tournois coinage was of slightly higher value than Melgorian in the late thirteenth and early fourteenth century. See Peter Spufford, *Handbook of Medieval Exchange* (London: Offices of the Royal Historical Society, 1986), 181.

[27]Dante Alighieri, *Hell* XV, 106–08, in *The Divine Comedy of Dante Alighieri*, trans. Jefferson Butler Fletcher (New York: Columbia University Press, 1931),

Dante further criticized the literary style of Jacopo da Lentino (d. ca. 1250), a notary of Emperor Frederick II, in *Purgatory*.[28] Echoing Dante's negative depiction of notaries, Boccaccio, in his first story of the *Decameron*, stated that a notary by the name of Ciappelletto would consider it a blight upon his honor if one of his legal documents were other than false.[29] Boccaccio may have had more cause than Dante to depict notaries in this fashion since he had been appointed early in life to apprenticeships in both canon law and commerce, where he would have had contact with notaries.[30] While Chaucer's "Clerk's Tale" does not specifically refer to notaries, and the notary in England was perceived more as a scribe than as a legal practitioner, he would share in negative associations. However, despite the dubious reputation of notaries in literature, Dante and Boccaccio did acknowledge that notaries were highly trained, educated men.

TYPES OF NOTARIES AND REGISTERS

Notaries had various official titles, according to the public authority by which they were licensed to practice. They usually attached their titles after their names at the end of the documents they wrote. Common designations in the case of Montpellier were those of "royal notary" or "public notary"; occasionally, a notary held the title of "notary of the bailiff's court."[31] Ecclesiastical authorities could also license notaries.

---

68. Paget Toynbee, *Concise Dictionary of Proper Names and Notable Matters in the Works of Dante* (New York: Phaeton Press, 1968)], identified this notary as Latini whom Dante named in *Hell* XV, 30 and 101. Brunetto Latini was associated with the Sodomites in Canto XV.

[28]Dante Alighieri, *Purgatory* XXIV, 56–59, in *The Divine Comedy of Dante Alighieri*, 267. Again Toynbee, *Concise Dictionary*, 312, identified the notary in question as Lentino.

[29]Giovanni Boccaccio, "First Story," *The Decameron*, trans. G. H. McWilliam (New York: Penguin Books, 1972), 70.

[30]Boccaccio showed no aptitude for these professions and instead turned to a literary career. See McWilliam, "Translator's Introduction," *The Decameron*, 21.

[31]A. M. Montpellier, II 2, Jean Grimaud: 1301–1302, fol. 74r; A. D. Hérault, II E 95/371, Jean Holanic: 1342, fols. 14v and 17r.

There were public notaries of bishops and apostolic (papal) and imperial notaries.[32] The variety of notarial titles provides an illustration of
the multitude of political influences in an urban crossroads such as
Montpellier. Each notary was an extension of the political authority
that authenticated his practice.

Most notarial registers were public registers; anyone could hire the
notary to record an act. The notary set up shop on a street corner, in a
marketplace, or in his atelier (workshop). He also moved about from
central square to stable to market, following business demand. During
the visitation of the Black Plague in 1348, there is even one tale of a
notary who climbed a tree to record, at a safe distance, the will of one
of his diseased clients. People came to notaries as their needs arose—
hence the randomness of the notarial record.

Occasionally, in the surviving notarial archives one finds registers
which are termed private. They were kept by notaries for a particular
individual or particular families and contained contracts related to the
business and lives of those clients. The acts of a private register generally extended over a series of years. Active businessmen with lots of
commercial and financial dealings may have found it useful to establish
a long-term relationship with a particular notary who became a close
confidant in their affairs. In the Montpellier notarial archive there sur-
vives the private register of the notary Guillaume Nogaret for the Cabanis
brothers, merchants and mercers, over the years 1337–42.[33] At the end
of the second half of the fourteenth century there are four private
registers for Montpellier.[34] They were written for the pepperer and spice
merchant Guillaume Basquèse; for Pons d'Arras, draper; for Jacques

---

[32]A. D. Hérault, II E 95/377, Bernard Gilles: 1347–48, fol. 300r and
A. D. Hérault, II E 95/369, Jean Holanie: 1333, fol. 25r. For mention of the
imperial notary, see A. D. Hérault, II E 95/370, Jean Holanie: 1336, fol. 11r.
There was licensing by the German emperor, as southern France, east of the
Rhône, was under imperial overlordship, though in the hands of the counts of
Provence and then the Angevin kings from the time of Charles of Anjou in
the 1260s.
[33]A. D. Hérault, II E 95/374, G. Nogaret.
[34]A. D. Hérault, II E 95/389, P. Bordon; II E 95/391, G. Bordon; II E
95/392, G. Bordon; II E 95/393, G. Bordon.

Jordan, merchant and money-changer, along with acts for Bernard Salamon, pepperer; and for Jean de Serrières, merchant.[35] The fifteenth century preserves additional private registers. There were private registers elsewhere in the south of France, as early as the thirteenth century in Perpignan.[36] The notary Jean Holanie did not leave any private registers; the acts of this book are from one of his public registers, of which there are five surviving for the first half of the fourteenth century. Many more public registers than private survive, and they present the reader with a great variety of evidence reflecting a diverse notarial clientele.

THE NOTARIAL CLIENTELE

The notary's clientele consisted of individuals—Christians and Jews, men and women—seeking a written record of the significant transactions of their lives: marriage contracts; last wills and testaments; resolutions of disputes; purchases, both large and small, of land, houses, cloth, food, and wine; apprenticeships; designations of representatives (*procuratores*) with varying legal mandates; and scheduling and refinancing of debt, to name but a portion of the myriad types of acts preserved in notarial registers.[37] The specialized personnel of international commerce and finance, such as merchants, money-changers, pepperers, mercers, and drapers, were represented among the notarial clientele, but so too were artisans and tradesmen, such as butchers, bakers, and shoemakers; also present were agricultural workers, royal servants, members of the nobility, and the clergy. Although most of a notary's

---

[35]Debra A. Salata's University of Minnesota dissertation (2003) focuses on Guillaume Basquèse: "Sugar and Spices: The Trade of Guillelmus Basquese in Late Medieval Mediterranean Europe."

[36]See Richard W. Emery, *The Jews of Perpignan in the Thirteenth Century: An Economic Study Based on Notarial Records* (New York: Columbia University Press, 1959).

[37]Jewish use of notaries was described by Emery, *The Jews of Perpignan.* On Jews and notaries, see also Robert I. Burns, *The Jews in the Notarial Culture: Latinate Wills in Mediterranean Spain, 1250–1350* (Berkeley-Los Angeles: University of California Press, 1996), and Joseph Shatzmiller, *Recherches sur la communauté juive de Manosque au Moyen Age, 1240–1329* (Paris: Mouton, 1973).

clients were Christians, in cities such as Montpellier, Jews also appeared. Minors or underage children, in the company of adults, can be
found entering into apprenticeship engagements. In southern Europe
all manner of individuals had recourse to the notary for legal record-
keeping. Both the humble and the wealthy and powerful figured among
the notary's clients. Notarial documents shed light on the economic,
social, and legal history of the wealthy in towns and villages but also of
those of artisanal and laboring background, for all but vagabonds and the
completely destitute might have occasion to come before the notary,
and even these representatives of the lowest rungs of the social ladder
might figure as recipients of philanthropy.

The order of contracts in the notarial registers was random since
they were recorded as clients appeared before the notary's stall or at his
house, or, on occasion, as they summoned him to their houses or elsewhere. A recognition of debt for grain for one party might follow a
contract commissioning construction in stone for another, with the next
in order a loan and the rental of a house. The juxtaposition of unre-
lated but consecutive acts often resulted in the participants of one act
serving as witnesses in a following or preceding act. The translated documents included in this book have been arranged thematically, by type
of document, but they were scattered throughout the register.

Jean Holanie's clientele ran the local social gamut. Everyone from
fishermen to wealthy foreign and native merchants, as well as nobility,
appeared before him to draw up contracts. Holanie's register contains
acts which belong to the ordinary functions of business and daily life.
For example, on 26 January 1328 the notary Holanie had quite a lot of
business, as revealed in the following chart (see Table 1). Eight different
sets of clients sought his services in nine separate acts. The first to walk
in was a weigher who apprenticed himself to another weigher to learn
the occupation of weights and measures, important in trade. In the second
act a man from the region of Béziers, a town sixty kilometers west of
Montpellier, recognized his debt for the purchase of wool cloth from a
local draper. Then came a moneyer who drafted a recognition of debt
for the acquisition of silk from a woman. The widow of a mercer purchased canvas from a merchant, using the same credit technique. Next,
the daughter of a silversmith contracted for her dowry with the man

she was to marry, a merchant. In the following act she confirmed to her mother that the latter had created a dowry. In the seventh contract her mother acknowledged her own debt for the part of the dowry still outstanding to her future son-in-law, the groom. Then a hospital administrator hired a friar as his procurator to represent him, and finally, on that same day in January, the daughter of a changer made a gift to her uncle, a merchant. Nine contracts on one day represent a significant workload for the notary Holanie.

Table 1
A (Busy) Day in the Life of the Medieval Notary Jean Holanie in 1328

TYPE OF CONTRACT	FIRST PARTY	SECOND PARTY
apprenticeship	weigher	weigher
recognition of debt for wool cloth	man of Béziers diocese	draper
recognition of debt for silk	moneyer	woman
recognition of debt for canvas	widow of mercer	merchant
dowry contract	daughter of silversmith	merchant/groom
confirmation of dowry contract	daughter of silversmith	mother
recognition of debt for dowry	mother of bride	groom
hire of a *procurator*	preceptor of hospital	friar
donatio inter vivos (gift)	daughter of changer	her uncle, a merchant

Holanie's acts are a window on the world in Montpellier, presenting the historian with a cross-section of life in the second quarter of the fourteenth century; herein lie their uses. Their limitations stem from the fact that no other registers survive from 1327–28, and only five of what must have been a much larger number of Holanie's registers in the whole of his notarial career are extant. Nonetheless, we come face to face with the daily life of Montpellier inhabitants and foreigners in passing in these acts (see Table 1). From the maritime partnership of several thousand royals[38] to the modest retail cloth sale or grape transaction, these acts are not especially significant in isolation, but when taken together they provide a valuable composite view of social and economic life. The very randomness of the records is useful as there seems to be no overriding agenda utilized in shaping a notarial register.

THE HOLANIE REGISTER

Jean Holanie's register for the year 1327–28 extends from 7 July 1327 to 3 April 1328. There were several forms of dating of documents in the Middle Ages which did not employ 1 January as the beginning of the new year. The year began in Montpellier on 25 March, a dating style termed the Incarnation or *calculus Florentinus* style. The dates in the Holanie register are thus labeled 1327 until almost the last acts. Dates in the transcriptions which follow use our modern dating style with the abbreviation n. s. (new style) after the date to indicate that the medieval dating practice has been converted to the modern calendar year.

Notaries might produce one or two registers of upwards of one hundred folios (two-sided pages) in one year.[39] Most were written on paper, as opposed to parchment, which was commonly used for charters. Holanie's register is a long one, running 151 folios; there is really no norm in length, as registers can be much shorter, sometimes longer. However, the register of 1327–28 contains over 860 acts, the largest number of any register surviving in the Montpellier notarial archives for the first half of the fourteenth century. Within all notarial registers—and the Holanie register is no exception—there are references to literally thousands of additional earlier acts which had a bearing on the contract at hand. Later insertions into the register added another layer of acts, often signaling the end of a contractual obligation (by acquittal or cancellation) and representing a subsequent agreement or acknowledgment of satisfaction by the parties to the acts. Thus a contract made one year might have a paragraph added a year later, stating that

---

[38]Royals were gold coins.
[39]Emery, *The Jews of Perpignan*, 6–8.

the original terms of the contract had been met. The single largest category of acts involved acquittals from obligations. Many were unspecified, but others cited specific items at issue. There were in the Holanie register, for example, eight acquittals for the payment of legacies of last wills and testaments. The register preserved three wills, one of which is reproduced below (Document 31). Of 294 acts relating to trade in the Holanie register, 271 entailed sales, debts, and acquittals. Contracts creating partnerships accounted for fifteen documents, and contracts hiring the transport of merchandise for another seven. Of the 210 acts which fell broadly in the category of credit and finance, sixty-seven were loans. There were ten marriage contracts, thirty-five apprenticeship contracts, and nineteen work contracts, as well as seven intermediate contracts involving both training and work. Real property transactions, divided between rural lands near the town and urban and suburban real estate, houses, and gardens, accounted for 131 acts.

Montpellier's ties with the surrounding countryside and the agricultural economy were very strong, as was the case with all medieval towns. Landholding was complex and multi-layered in the Middle Ages, involving outright sales (Document 32), but also rentals (Document 35), leases of land (Documents 36 and 37), exchanges (Document 38), sales of rights (usufruct) over land (Document 39), and even sharecropping (Document 40), to mention only those represented in the Holanie register. Land transactions often required the approval of family members (Document 34). Houses, both urban and suburban, gardens, fields, vineyards, and commercial property such as market tables were also involved.

Commerce—local, regional, and international—was represented in the Holanie register. The trade in animals of transport and burden was lively, with eleven horse sales, construed as recognitions of debt (Document 11) and twenty-three contracts regarding asses and mules. Local agricultural needs accounted for some of these, but overland regional and international trade also required animals as pack animals, for personal transportation and for carts. The remains of slaughtered sheep (Document 17), beans, fleeces, rabbit pelts, and olive oil reflected a local and regional trade, while salted meat (Document 13), books (Document 20), and grain (Document 16) probably figured in an international arena as did silk (Document 15), linen, and wool cloth (Document 12).[40]

The production of wine was significant in the region of Montpellier in the Middle Ages, as it is today and had been in Roman times.[41] Grape-growing and wine production are reflected in the twenty-four acts relating to the sale or certification of the sale of vineyards, an example of which occurs below in Document 33. All manner of inhabitants dabbled in vineyards, as one might expect in an economy which remained close to the land. Montpellier in the mid-thirteenth century was said to contain some six thousand cultivators.[42] We also know that self-respecting inhabitants placed great store by their wine.

The trade in grapes appeared in the register as a futures operation, with the sale of grapes on the vine to be delivered at the next harvest.[43] An example has been included in Document 21. The notary carefully identified the provenance of the grapes because the vineyard of origin would affect the quality of the wine. Of thirty-eight acts dealing with

---

[40]Of thirty-six acts relating to the sale of grain, four mentioned the Byzantine Empire as provenance. An additional sixteen acts mentioned wheat, with one wheat import from the Byzantine Empire.

[41]For background on vineyards in the region of medieval Montpellier, see Kathryn Reyerson, "Land, Houses and Real Estate Investment: A Study of the Notarial Property Transactions, 1293–1348," *Studies in Medieval and Renaissance History* VI (old ser. XVI) (1983): 37–112, and "Commerce and Society in Montpellier: 1250–1350," (Diss., Yale University, 1974), I, Chapter 3.8: "Grapes and Wine."

[42]Those selling or certifying vineyard sales included merchants, cultivators, wives of cultivators and a wood merchant, a draper, a butcher, a shoemaker, a weigher, a wax maker, a table holder, a grain merchant, the wife of a grain merchant, a brother and knight of St. John of Jerusalem, the wife of a mercer, a fisherman, and a leather merchant. Those buying vineyards included bakers, a secondhand clothes dealer, a wood merchant, a wine merchant, a leather merchant, the wife of a leather merchant, a barber, cultivators, a candlemaker, a flour maker, a goldsmith, a grain merchant, the wife of a wood merchant, a man of a nearby village, Loupian, and a leathersmith of Sommières, about twenty-five kilometers to the northeast of Montpellier.

[43]On the wine trade in medieval Europe, see Roger Dion, *Histoire de la vigne et du vin en France des origines au XIXe siècle* (Paris: 1959, rpt. Flammarion, 1977).

the purchase of grapes, some involved a specified number of measures, the *saumata* being the common measure of volume, whereas the remaining ones simply delivered all the fruits of a specific vineyard. The town government, or consulate, of Montpellier safeguarded the marketability of local grapes, prohibiting the import of any wine not from grapes of the vineyards of Montpellier inhabitants.[44] Montpellier was renowned for its spiced wine production, and liqueurs, flavored with spices, were a local specialty. There was demand for these wines as far afield as England, where the so-called "*giroflé*" (*garhilfilatum*) and claret were ordered for the king.[45] Specialty wines were the niche available to the wine of Montpellier in the context of international trade.

The cloth trade, illuminated by the Holanie register, included a variety of fabrics: silks, wool cloth, linen, and cotton.[46] Wool cloth was the type most commonly traded. There were forty-six sales of wool cloth, all construed as recognitions of debt. Among the sellers were twelve merchants and thirty-two wholesalers, most of them drapers. The bulk of the buyers were foreigners from small towns surrounding Montpellier.[47] Prices were quoted in real coins as opposed to money of account (a system of computation with the denominations of pennies, shillings, and pounds), a more common practice overall in the notarial registers.[48] Only small sums were involved in each purchase, suggesting

---

[44]This regulation dates from 1317. Letters of Philip V, king of France, had carried a similar order in 1316, reviving a history of protectionism for Montpellier wine which goes back to Philip IV in 1294 and 1299 regulations, in particular. In 1300 Philip IV purchased about 150 hectoliters which were sent to Paris.

[45]*Calendar of Liberate Rolls*, IV (London, 1959) and V (London, 1961), for specific sales.

[46]On the medieval cloth trade in Montpellier, see Kathryn Reyerson, "Le rôle de Montpellier dans le commerce des draps de laine avant 1350," *Annales du Midi* 94 (1982): 17–40.

[47]In addition, cloth sellers included one member of the artisanal trades and one legal specialist. Buyers counted two wholesalers, six from the nobility and bourgeoisie, two ecclesiastics, one woman, eight tradesmen, one member of the food trades and one agriculturalist.

[48]For further information on coinage and money, see Kathryn Reyerson, *Business, Banking and Finance in Medieval Montpellier* (Toronto: The Pontifical Institute of Mediaeval Studies, 1985), especially Appendix 2.

that people of the region came to the large town, Montpellier, to buy
for individual or family needs. A lot of the cloth sold was made region-
ally, probably procured by Montpellier drapers at the Languedocian
fairs of Pézenas, Montagnac, and Villevayrac. Of all the registers extant
before 1350, the Holanie register of 1327–28 reveals most about this
regional trade.

The foreign presence in Montpellier trade is significant throughout the Middle Ages. Foreigners using Montpellier in 1327 included
merchants of Narbonne who entered into *commenda* partnership contracts to finance their participation in the Levant trade.[49] Narbonnais
merchants and their ships used the international port of Aigues-Mortes,
the principal Mediterranean port in the vicinity of Montpellier. Of the
fourteen *commenda* contracts extant for 1327–28, four were arranged
exclusively among Narbonnais and concerned the transport of wool cloth
to the Levant on ships anchored at Aigues-Mortes. Document 1 provides an example. Among these maritime partnerships were large investments of over two thousand gold royals.

Financial operations were always abundant in notarial registers since
proof of obligation was of foremost importance. International trade
was financed in part through foreign exchange. Foreign exchange contracts (Document 23) often involved foreigners like the Salati of Lérida,
who borrowed money from a man of Montpellier with the promise to
repay him in another coinage in Valencia in Spain. The high and
mighty along with the meek sought to make ends meet through borrow-
ing, and so loans were another prominent fixture of notarial registers
(Document 22). The guaranteeing of obligations (Document 25), the
transfer of credits and indebtedness (Document 26), and negotiation of
compromise over debts (Document 27) also figured frequently among
the reasons for going to the notary. The notarial contract legally reinforced any obligation.

The Holanie register contains a great variety of contractual operations and a diverse clientele of participants. Family, business, and social
relations emerge from the notarial acts. It is possible to analyze the
mechanisms of trade and finance in the urban context and to trace

---

[49]On commercial partnerships, see Reyerson, *Business, Banking and Finance.*

some aspects of the agricultural economy, as the rural world surrounding Montpellier was closely connected to the town. Indeed, urban-rural exchange remains one of the hallmarks of the medieval economy.

NOTARIAL DOCUMENTS

The written contracts of notaries were known also as instruments *(instrumenta)* or acts *(acta)*. The notarial instrument might be a will, a contract, an act of litigation, an emancipation, an appointment to office, an acquittal, a statement or a letter of one king or another—all solemnly registered by the notary in the presence of witnesses. The number of witnesses varied according to the type of act, wills requiring greater numbers than sales of goods, for example. Roman law mandated seven witnesses in wills, but medieval notarial wills generally carried fewer. Three or more witnesses were common in English wills.[50] The notary's instruments or recorded acts in the minute book were proof of the validity of a contract and could be used as such in a court of law. Written proof only became widely accepted in the thirteenth century in Europe, slowly replacing oath-sayers, the duel or trial by combat, and the ordeals that had been used as a means of proof for centuries. Contractual obligations of the parties to the act were set out and were validated and enforced by notarial contracts.[51] Under Roman and medieval law, a contract by itself could be oral, but the notarial record offered a convenient means of proof.[52] The notary's register or cartulary served the purpose of a much expanded registry of public deeds, preserving notations of engagements for which written proof might be needed in the future.

Notaries used at least three types of recording techniques: the brief note *(breve)*, the minute *(nota)*, and the extended act *(grossus)*.[53] The

---

[50]We owe this insight to Joel Rosenthal.

[51]Clifford R. Backman, "Private Law in Fourteenth-Century Montpellier: The Notarial Register of Guillaume Nogaret," master's thesis, University of Minnesota (1983), 29.

[52]Backman, "Private Law," 30–31.

[53]Herlihy, *Pisa in the Early Renaissance*, 2–4, has more fully described the drafting process.

brief note might be written on a scrap of paper with a few details of
the contractual arrangement; because of its informality, but also because of the fact that it was generally a loose sheet of paper, few brief
notes have survived. A more complete version of the contract, called a
minute, contained the specific information of the contract: the names
of participants, agents, or procurators; notation of sale items, quota-
tions of prices (although rarely of the quantity of goods); mention of contiguous geographic coordinates in land transactions; repayment data; and
so on. The notary carefully wrote out the date and place the contract
was established, and the witnesses, including himself, to the agreement.
However, in order to conserve space and time, he used a short-hand
method of abbreviations and *et cetera* clauses, replacing the formulaic
and legalistic clauses which were common knowledge within the notarial tradition, prompting at least one French scholar to write an article,
"God Preserve Us from the *Et Cetera* of the Notary."[54] Minutes were
generally bound together in registers in chronological order. Holanie's
minutes had abbreviations but also contained sufficient information
for him to draw up an extended form of the transaction (*grossus*) at the
request of one or more of the participants in the act. Moreover, a
complete, unabbreviated act was occasionally included in the notarial
register. The first act of the Holanie register, a sale of real estate
(Document 32), is an example of a contract written out in full, several
folios in length.

   If the parties to a contract wanted their own copies of an instrument in order to have legal proof of contractual obligations, the
notary would produce an extended act from the data of the minutes,
with the legal formulas unabbreviated. The notary then made a notation
in his register that he had extracted the act (*"Extractum est instrumentum"*). The extended act was again subject, as was the brief note, to
uncertain survival because it was usually not preserved in an official

---

[54]Auguste Dumas, "Dieu nous garde de l'*et cetera* du notaire," *Mélanges
Paul Fournier* (Paris: Recueil Sirey, 1929), 153–69. On clauses in notarial acts,
see Peter Riesenberg, "Roman Law, Renunciations and Business in the Twelfth
and Thirteenth Centuries," in *Essays in Medieval Life and Thought Presented in
Honor of Austin Patterson Evans*, ed. John Hine Mundy et al. (New York:
Columbia University Press, 1955), 207–25.

notarial register, but rather by individuals; however, extended acts on parchment can be found in some European archival collections.[55] Technically speaking, the notary's register itself was adequate proof of contractual obligations, though there is no recorded instance of a register's use in a court of law. Nevertheless, it was this feature of the notarial instrument—its validity as proof in a court of law—which accounts for the remarkable survival of notarial registers from the High and Late Middle Ages in southern Europe.[56]

A notarial contract is divided into three parts: *protocol, corpus,* and *eschatocol.* The act begins with the protocol, which includes such terms as the date of the contract and the governing authority or jurisdiction under which the contract was made. The very first clause records the date of the contract, the *datum* clause. In a fully extracted contract, this clause might state: "In the year of the Incarnation of the Lord one thousand three hundred twenty-seven and on the seventh day of the month of July." The notary would write out this clause in full for the first act in his register and possibly for the first act at the beginning of a new year if his register contained acts from several years. It is unlikely, however, that the notary would write out this *datum* clause for each and every act. Instead, he would use a much shorter phrase, "in the year stated above." Immediately following the *datum* clause, the notary acknowledged the governmental authority or jurisdiction under which the contract was made. Notation might be made of the king's name and regnal year, or the year of office of a pope or bishop. If, for some reason, the *datum* clause were unclear or illegible, this notation might also be used to date the contract approximately. In the acts of the Holanie register, the protocol gives the date, according to the Incarnation of the Lord in the Christian calendar and the name of the reigning king of France, who was first Charles IV (1322–28), the last of the Capetian kings, and then

---

[55]Some extended acts were also collected in registers. It is sometimes difficult for the historian to discover the exact wording of the phrases which the *et cetera* clauses replaced. Phraseology differed from notary to notary. Each notary might use *et cetera* clauses in a different manner.

[56]On the notarial register as legal proof, see Herlihy, *Pisa in the Early Renaissance,* 1–20.

Philip VI of Valois (1328–50), who succeeded him.[57] There was no reference to holders of local municipal office.

The *corpus* or body of the contract contains the terms of the agreement. It begins with the first names and surnames of the parties to the contract, who were usually further identified by place of origin and occupation or legal status. For example, "I, Pontius Salati, merchant of Lérida" (Document 23). Next, the reason for the contract is stated. In Pontius Salati's case "by reason of exchange" (*pro cambio*), that is, he was arranging an exchange of one coinage for another with an extension of credit as part of the bargain. Loans were drafted as recognitions of debt "by reason of a loan" (*causa mutui*) (Document 22). One party to the contract might be selling something to a second party, or hiring a second party, or might be apprenticing himself or herself to a second party, and so on.

The *corpus* of the contract also includes the exact conditions under which the contract would be carried out: payment terms; payment dates; descriptions of property; descriptions of specific obligations owed by each party; and provisions for the legal enforcement of the obligations of the agreement, whatever it was. Contingencies might be invoked to invalidate or modify the stated obligations: bad harvests, coinage devaluations, robbery on the highways or piracy at sea, even disputed claims to property.[58] Spiritual oaths and promises to pay figured among the conditions, as did Roman law renunciations.

A common renunciation offered legal protection to women by prohibiting them from assuming liability for another's debt (*senatusconsultum Velleianum*). Women needed to be freed from constraints on their ability to manage their business and engage themselves on behalf

---

[57]Beginning in 1282, the king of France required that his name, rather than that of the king of Majorca, appear on notarial contracts in Montpellier. Holanie's acts carried an indication of the king of France's reign in the *datum* clause.

The kingdom of Aragon-Majorca had been divided among the heirs of Jacme I in 1276, and Montpellier had gone with the cadet branch of the family who were kings of Majorca. On the history of the Capetian kings, see Elizabeth M. Hallam, *Capetian France, 987–1328* (London and New York: Longman), 1980.

[58]Backman, "Private Law," 35–36.

of others. Hence the renunciation of this protection. Another common renunciation required the counting out of money and protected debtors and borrowers from being required to repay more than they owed (*exceptio non numeratae pecuniae*). Early legal historians of Roman law renunciations argued that the notaries padded their acts with *pro forma* clauses that were really meaningless. More recent interpretations of the renunciations suggest that they were necessary to ensure individual contractual freedom.[59] Only in this way, in an environment where risk-taking was possible, could medieval business develop and prosper.

The legal jurisdictions under which contracts were drawn and before which any disputes would be settled were often clearly spelled out in the notarial contracts. For the south of France, courts of voluntary jurisdiction called "rigorous seals" (*seaux rigoureux*) were established by the king of France in the thirteenth century, subsequent to his victory in the Albigensian Crusade against Cathar heretics and his acquisition of southern French lands.[60] The court of the Little Seal (*Petit Scel*) was established by the king of France in Montpellier shortly after his acquisition of the episcopal quarter of the town in 1293. Another such court in the south of France was the Court of Conventions (*Cour des Conventions*) in Nîmes. These courts sought to dispense a rapid justice essential to medieval business on the basis of a commercial law that had developed in an urban context and was often quite distinct from rural, seigneurial, and feudal law.[61]

The notarial contract was generally abbreviated with *et cetera* clauses, which would replace the formulaic language appropriate to the type of contract. Abbreviations were common for the conditions of the contract

---

[59]On Roman law renunciations, see Riesenberg, "Roman Law, Renunciations and Business," 207–25.

[60]These courts were modeled on the Wardens' Court at the Champagne fairs, the most famous medieval fairs, attracting merchants from northern Europe and the Mediterranean world, in an annual cycle of fairs in the towns of Troyes, Provins, Lagny, and Bar-sur-Aube.

[61]From as early as the eleventh century, merchants had required efficient courts in order to resolve their disputes so that they could be on their way. These commercial courts were termed "piepowder" courts to reflect the fact that the feet of traveling merchant litigants were often dusty.

and might encompass a spiritual oath or a promise to pay. Roman law renunciations appeared frequently among the abbreviated phrases of notarial minutes. Legal jurisdictions for the contracts were often signaled by abbreviations as well.

The *eschatocol* (ending or conclusion of the contract) provided the place where the contract was written, a list of witnesses to the contract, and the notarial sign or signature. The *eschatocol* might also include the date if it were not in the *protocol*. The phrase stating where the contract was written is generally straightforward. It sometimes contains an additional statement regarding the jurisdiction of the contract, such as "in the king's section" (*parte regia*) of the town. Such a designation might be particularly important when jurisdictions overlapped or towns were divided among several jurisdictions, as was the case with Montpellier where there were two quarters, Montpellier and Montpelliéret, under separate jurisdiction of the secular lord and the bishop, respectively.[62]

Witnesses validated the contract and could be called on to testify to the contractual obligations in the case of a (later) dispute. Witnesses might be relatives of the parties to the contract, or prominent people of the town, or other notaries and scribes of the notarial workshop. They could be drawn from the individuals accompanying the parties to the act but also from those persons waiting in line at the notary's stall or simply standing nearby. The parties to a contract might later appear as witnesses to a consecutive contract made by those men who were witnesses for them. Clients might have milled around the notary's stall after their own business was completed and thus have been available to serve as witnesses for several acts. Generally, witnesses were identified by place of origin and occupation, just as were the parties to the contract. Witnesses were generally men. As a rule, in southern Europe, women could represent themselves in court, but they tended not to act as notarial witnesses, though they could be called upon in an inquest to offer testimony along with their male counterparts.[63] It is important for

---

[62]See Reyerson, *Business, Banking and Finance.*

[63]Medieval women's legal status varied over the centuries and from territory to territory. For examples of female witnesses in an inquest, see Kathryn L. Reyerson, "Public and Private Space in Medieval Montpellier: The Bon Amic Square," *The Journal of Urban History* 24 (1997): 3–27.

the historian not to overlook the witness list, as it may provide insight into networks of personal relationships among notarial clients or reveal the presence at the time of the establishment of a contract of individuals whose connection to a business deal might otherwise escape notice. In the case of brokers, their appearance on witness lists often provides the only link to their involvement in the process of doing business.[64]

After the witness list, the notary added his own name, often including his official title. In the acts of this book, the notary identified himself: "And I, Jean Holanie, public royal notary of Montpellier" or "royal notary of the king of France."[65] The notary might also append his notarial sign, unique to himself, to the document. Figure 1 shows the notarial sign of Holanie.

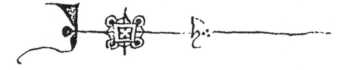

Figure 1. Notarial sign of Jean Holanie.

Finally, the notary might add a clause (*Extractum est instrumentum*) indicating that the contract had been fully written out or extended, eliminating any abbreviations or *et cetera* clauses, for one or more of the parties to the contract. The notary did not extend a contract, producing a full form of the document without abbreviations, unless specifically requested to do so. For one thing, the more he wrote, the higher his fees for his clients. Moreover, not every contract was produced in extended form, since the notary's minutes of the contract, contained in the notarial register, could provide legal proof of the existence of the contract. The notary himself could testify to the contractual obligations even in the absence of the parties to the contract or of the witnesses.[66]

Some contracts in the form of minutes in a notarial register were formally cancelled after fulfillment of the terms of obligation. The

---

[64]See Reyerson, *The Art of the Deal.*
[65]A. D. Hérault, II E 95/368-II, E 95/372, for Holanie's titles.
[66]Backman, "Private Law," 24–25.

notary used various notations to cancel a contract in a register. Sometimes an "X" or parallel lines were drawn through the text, though the
meaning of barred acts is not always clear and might vary from notary
to notary and from place to place.[67] As noted above, in other cases the
notary added a paragraph at the end of the contract to signal cancellation and satisfaction of the terms. If necessary, the paragraph would
be squeezed in between the lines at the bottom of the contract, above
or after the extraction clause if it was present. This cancellation paragraph included its own witness list, presumably because the parties to
the contract either had again appeared before the notary for the contract cancellation, or had sent their representatives, or had requested
the notary to act as their intermediary. There is no way to determine
whether the parties to the contract appeared before the notary for the
contract cancellation if the notary merely drew an "X" or lines through
the text of the contract. Furthermore, just because a notarial contract
carried no indication of cancellation did not mean that its terms had
gone unsatisfied. It was not uncommon to find that the notary drew up
a separate act of cancellation which may have been recorded in a different notarial register altogether; such a cancellation may have even been
drawn up by a different notary.[68] The extended form of the notarial
contract, often written on parchment, would normally be torn up in
the case of cancellation of the obligations in the contract, generally
upon their fulfillment. This practice may account for the limited
survival of the extended forms of contract, beyond the vicissitudes
attached to their being in the safe-keeping of individuals, rather than a
notarial atelier.

CONCLUSION

For the reader interested in using notarial registers, there is more
to master than the rudiments provided in this introduction to medieval
notaries and their acts. Plate 1 on p. x of this book features a photo of

---

[67]Herlihy, *Pisa in the Early Renaissance*, 6–8.
[68]For a specific acquittal, see A. D. Hérault, II E 95/368, Jean Holanie:
1327–28, fol. 23r, translated in this book as Document 24.

the first folio of acts of the 1327–28 register of Jean Holanie. The language as well as the handwriting, along with the shorthand of abbreviations and legal formulas, provide challenges to readers. Researchers must study the paleography of notarial hands before it is possible to read the acts themselves. They must familiarize themselves with the notary's abbreviated style of formulaic medieval Latin. The modern reader will find that the translations included here, reflecting the original medieval Latin of the documents, are a bit stilted and technical at times, just as modern legal documents may appear to the layperson today. With time and effort readers can become conversant with these rich sources for the exploration of medieval social, economic, and legal history. We invite you to become acquainted with this historical evidence in the following documents in translation.

SELECTED DOCUMENTS IN TRANSLATION FROM THE HOLANIE REGISTER

EDITORS' NOTE

The forty documents included here represent the range of engagements recorded by the notary Holanie. Most are in the form of minutes with abbreviations of familiar legal formulas, and most are quite short. However, the first act of the Holanie register, a sale of land and houses (Document 32), has been included to provide readers with an example of a fully drafted contract, with formulas written out. Another very lengthy act is the last will and testament (Document 31), provided in lightly excerpted form to illustrate the extraordinary care taken by some individuals in preparation for their deaths. The dowry, marriage, and augmentation contract (Document 28) is also without abbreviation. Not all of the acts in the register are legible, and some of them have been eaten away by worms over time. The documents included are in good condition, but there are still times when the notary failed to fill in the whole act; this will be noted as an ellipsis: . . . . References to different types of coinage appear in these forty acts, as do numerous technical terms. The reader can consult the Glossary for definitions. The documents have been organized thematically with short introductions, though they appear randomly in the register. Their place in the register is indicated by the folio numbers and the date of the transaction. Personal names have been left in the Latin of the original documents.

31

BUSINESS TECHNIQUES

Merchants and the general populace in the Middle Ages used a whole host of contractual agreements to further their commercial and financial interests. Many of these contracts have roots in Roman law; others are of medieval invention. They include a variety of partnership arrangements, delegations of authority in agency or procuration, transport contracts for the shipment of goods, the hiring of services, and the apprenticeship of young workers. Notarial business contracts underpinned maritime and land trade and local artisan industry.

Commenda Partnership Contract

The *commenda* was a medieval partnership contract not derived from Roman legal precedents.[1] This contract was of Mediterranean origin with likely influences from both Islamic and Jewish precedents. Appearing in the tenth century, the *commenda*—the name of which is untranslatable—was a form of one-time business partnership in which an investor or investors put up the capital for a business venture and another partner contributed his labor and did whatever traveling was needed for the venture. Often the profits from the venture were then split, three-fourths to the investing partner(s), and one-fourth to the traveling partner(s). The investing partner incurred all the financial risk of the business venture; the traveling partner incurred all the physical risks of the enterprise. Each *commenda* contract could alter the relationship between the partners and change the terms of the business venture. For the most part, every *commenda* contract stated the names of the parties and their relationship to the business venture, the terms of the venture, the destination of the traveling partner, and the terms for the distribution of profits from the enterprise. A *commenda* contract did not usually state the time within which the work was to be accomplished. The time limits were usually open-ended because of the many delays and risks, such as weather or piracy, which could affect the traveling partner and the business at hand.

---

[1] See John H. Pryor, "The Origins of the Commenda Contract," *Speculum* 52 (1977): 5–37.

A distinction can be made between land and maritime *commenda* contracts. The *commenda* contract below deals with international maritime trade in the hands of business partners from Narbonne. The traveling partner was leaving from the Mediterranean port of Aigues-Mortes in southern France and traveling by ship to Romania (that is, the Byzantine Empire). *Commenda* contracts are particularly fruitful for scholars studying medieval commerce. The contracts provide insight into the business and social relationships between the parties and reveal the commodities and luxury goods of exchange. Such acts may also provide information on medieval trade routes and on exchange rates between different coinages.

1. *Commenda* **Contract:** Folio 12r (recto)–12v (verso), dated 28 July 1327:

In the above year and on the twenty-eighth day of the month of July, Lord Charles etc., I, Guillelmus Bocuti, merchant of Narbonne, etc. acknowledge to you, Bernardus Assaudi, merchant of Narbonne, present and stipulating and receiving these things on behalf of you and Thomas Mossani and Bertrandus Assaudi the younger, merchants of Narbonne and your associates, and on behalf of your men and their men, that I truly have had and received, and henceforth have and hold, from you and in your name and in the name of your said associates, in *comanda*[2] and by reason of and in the name of a true and legitimate *comanda*, namely: 50 *l.p.t.*, invested at my wish in good woolen cloth and linen, worth that much, which I will take and carry with me on this next journey to Romania in which I am going and propose to go. Concerning which I renounce etc. And I promise and acknowledge to you, stipulating and receiving as above, whereby I, with said *comanda* and with the merchandise purchased and to be purchased concerning the same in this next journey to Romania and in whatever other areas not prohibited by our lord, king of the Franks, and by our lord, the most high Pontiff, and by the lords of other territories and places, will market, profit from, and

---

[2]The local spelling of *commenda* was *comanda*.

negotiate, as much on the sea as on land and in those goods in which I will be best able, and as God will guide me through danger, moreover, and at your risk, remote, known, and unknown. Also, moreover, I will have a fourth part of all profits and returns which I, as long as I will hold said *comanda*, will earn and acquire with the same aforesaid *comanda* and with the merchandise purchased and to be purchased concerning the same, and you and your said associates [will have] the remaining three parts of the aforesaid profit and return. I will give to you or your said associates a good and legal reckoning, and a full and strict account when the aforesaid journey has been made. And also I promise and acknowledge to you, stipulating and receiving as above, and through you, to your said associates, and to your men and theirs, that I will return and restore to you stipulating or to your said associates or to others of theirs or yours, or to a reliable agent or *procurator* of yours, in peace and without argument, moreover, with the good will of God and with the distant and diminishing [luck] of the pirates, the entire aforesaid *comanda* along with the said three parts of the entire profit invested in good merchandise, namely: in the port of Aigues-Mortes, completely, on demand, once the trip has been made, etc., with all restitution of losses etc. Concerning which etc. For which etc. I obligate etc. myself and all my present and future goods. I renounce, etc. I promise through faith, etc.

And fully, I, said Bernardus Assaudi, in my own name and in the name of my said associates, from whom I promise to ratify under the obligation of all my present and future property, I wish and expressly concede to you, the said Guillelmus Bocuti, present, etc. that you will have and can and ought to have an entire fourth part of the whole aforesaid gain and profit, without any objection by me and my said associates, whatsoever.

And subsequently, I, Bernardus Franci, merchant of Narbonne, having certified etc. for each and all the aforesaid things promised, considered, and completed by the aforesaid Guillelmus Bocuti etc., constitute myself along with said Guillelmus

Bocuti and together as a faithful pledgor, principal debtor, and surety to you, said Bernardus Assaudi, present and stipulating these things on your behalf and for your said associates etc. I obligate etc. myself and all my present and future property under my requested good faith, fully. I renounce etc.

Enacted in Montpellier. These are the witnesses: Raymundus de Piniano, Bernardus de Piniano, brothers, merchants of Narbonne, Guillelmus Holanie the younger, cleric of Montpellier, and I, Johannes Holanie etc.

The instrument was extracted for said Bernardus Assaudi and his associates.

Hiring of Legal Representation

Procuration or proxy was one means of legal representation in the Middle Ages. The need for representation in business dealings has a history preceding the medieval era. Roman law had an institution of *procurator* in terms of business representative or manager, but the term could also be applied to someone holding public office. A medieval *procurator* could represent his principal with a general mandate to act or be restricted by his appointment to operations within a narrow sphere. Procuration provided an essential tool for conducting business at a distance. The first contract below involves ecclesiastics instituting procuration for representation in a particular lawsuit with other churchmen; the second concerns a pepperer of Montpellier, a member of a prestigious occupation, who hired a spice merchant to seek reimbursement from the *vicarius* of Montels, a town of the Montpellier hinterland.

2. **Procuration**: Folio 58v, dated 17 October 1327:
  In the year and on the day aforesaid, we, Bernardus de Bociassis, canon of Maguelone and archdeacon of Posquières [present-day Vauvert] in the church of Nîmes, etc. make etc. our special and general *procuratores* those prudent men below for the purpose written below: Lord Pontius de Olargio, canon of Maguelone, prior of the church of Saint-George and Lord Pontius de Olargio the younger, canon of Maguelone, and

Lord Stephanus Amancii, prior of Prades, legitimately absent as much as present and bearers of this public instrument, and Lord Petrus Raymundi of Boisseron, canon of Maguelone, present and receiving, together and each of them individually etc., namely: to appear for us and in our name and to defend us as much in the presence of the Reverend Father in Christ, Lord Andreas, by divine compassion, Bishop of Maguelone, as in the presence of those judges, ecclesiastical or secular, ordinary or extraordinary, delegated or subdelegated, or in the presence of whatever other magistrates and persons by whatever power they adjudicate and in whatever place and in whatever court, ecclesiastical or temporal; namely: that the case or lawsuit which exists between the Lord Provost and the chapter of Maguelone on one side and us on the other side may be overturned and also to undertake and propose, over and above the said case, etc. and to hear whatever other summation or summations and each and all definitions, settlements and investigations etc. and to compromise with penalties or without penalties and finally, generally etc.

Enacted in Montpellier. These are the witnesses: Lord Raymundus Capioni, priest, Bernardus Ariberti, Petrus Roca, *domicelli,* and I etc.

This instrument was extracted.

3. **Procuration**: Folio 66r–v, dated 29 October 1327:

In the above year and on the twenty-ninth day of the month of October, Lord Charles [reigning], I, Bertrandus Vallete, pepperer of Montpellier, etc. make etc. my special and general *procurator* Bartholmeus de Rohergue, spice merchant of Montpellier, legitimately absent etc. for the purpose written below, namely: to seek etc. each and all my debts and credits in which Lord Michael Pasturelli, *vicarius* of Saint-Sauveur of Montels, is obligated to me with charters or without charters and for whatever reason or cause and to make recognitions, acquittals, and agreements with said Lord Michael Pasturelli not to seek those things which my said *procurator* recovers

from the aforesaid. And in addition to act and appear for me
and in my name and for the aforesaid and by an action of these
against and opposed to said Lord Michael Pasturelli and
against his property before whatever judges etc. And to compromise with penalties or without penalties and finally, generally
etc. Settled etc. relieving etc. establishing etc.

Enacted in Montpellier. These are the witnesses: Johannes
de Ruthena, pepperer, Henricus de Lozena, mercer, inhabitants of Montpellier, and I etc.

The instrument was extracted.

Transport

Transport contracts were agreements in which merchants arranged
for the transport of their merchandise to a distant place. The trans-
porter pledged on his honor to carry out the terms of the contract.
Transport contracts specified the goods to be transported, the destination of the goods, and the time limit within which the contract had
to be carried out. These contracts can provide information on the
types of merchandise available, market areas, and business relationships. They do not usually cite the cost of the transport itself. In
general, luxury goods formed the basis of overland transport. Bulk
items such as food stuffs were too heavy to transport over long distances; moreover, the cost would have been prohibitive. Most transport
out of Montpellier was directed north to markets like Paris and the
Champagne fairs, as Montpellier served as an entry point into France
and the North for Mediterranean goods. Transport east and west from
Montpellier might be overland, but could also be by sea in a coastal
carrying trade.

4.   **Transport Contract**: Folio 55v, dated 12 October 1327:
In the year and on the day aforesaid, I, Petrus Coste of
Le Caylar, in the diocese of Lodève, etc. acknowledge etc. to
you, Arnaudus Rosselli, merchant of Lérida, *procurator* etc., of
Petrus Salati, present, etc. that I had from you in Montpellier
etc., namely: thirteen bales of white cordovan leather etc. which

etc. I will transport to Paris, unburdened, discharged, and free
from all tolls, without being untied etc. within twenty-three
days from today etc. I obligate etc. myself and all my present
and future property. I renounce etc. through faith etc. acknowledging etc. that I have had from you etc., by reason of
the transport of the above etc. And, in full, I, Johannes Bastide,
innkeeper of Montpellier, having certified etc., constitute myself
along with the said Petrus Coste and together as faithful pledger
and principal debtor publicly, and surety, with the exception
of fire and water, to you, the said Arnaudus Rosselli, the aforesaid *procurator*, present. For which etc. I obligate etc. myself and
all my present and future property. I renounce etc. through
faith etc.

   Enacted in Montpellier. These are the witnesses: Raymundus Jaolli of the said Le Caylar, Johannes Britonis, furrier
of Montpellier, and I etc.

Apprenticeship and Work

   Medieval industry and many occupations were organized hierar-
chically, with masters at the top, then journeymen, and finally appren-
tices. The training of young people as artisans in trades and crafts and
as merchants and financiers often took the form of apprenticeship.[3]
Trades ranging from elite mercantile occupations such as pepperers, and
drapers, to highly skilled artisans such as goldsmiths, to makers of the
necessities of life such as bakers and shoemakers all used apprenticeships to train young workers. Young women and men were generally
apprenticed in the life phase of adolescence for terms of instruction
running from a year to upwards of ten or twelve years. Apprenticeship
contracts in the Holanie register often show one or both parents apprenticing a son or daughter, but a boy who was of the legal age of fourteen could also apprentice himself, though usually this was done in

---

   [3]See the special issue of the *Journal of Family History*, 17 (1992), on *The
Evolution of Adolescence in Europe*, ed. Barbara A. Hanawalt. On apprenticeship in this volume, see Kathryn Reyerson, "The Adolescent Apprentice/Worker
in Medieval Montpellier," 353–70.

collaboration with family members or friends if the apprentice were that young. There are no examples of young women acting alone. Apprenticeship contracts might include a fee paid by the parent/parents to the master for the instruction of a child. A contract of an intermediate sort might include instruction with some minimal salary once the child was able to work independently for the master. In all cases the master was obliged by the contract to maintain the apprentice in the necessities of life: shelter, food, and clothing.

Work contracts were construed in a fashion similar to that of apprenticeship contracts, as a kind of self-rental, with the difference that some arrangement for salary for work accomplished in a particular trade would be included. Work in a particular occupation was often governed by guild regulations (statutes) if the particular craft was incorporated with official recognition from a political authority.

5. **Apprenticeship Contract**: Folio 74v, dated 11 November 1327:

In the year and on the day aforesaid, I, Guillelmus de Remis, shoemaker of Montpellier, bestow and contract in apprenticeship and study my son Julianus to you, Guillelmus Hospitalis, shoemaker of said place, present and receiving, namely: for four years from today etc. to stay with you and to learn your trade of shoemaking and [to do] all other of your legitimate and honest biddings as much within the town of Montpellier as without throughout all the said time. Moreover, you, promising etc. on the basis of the standing agreement between me and you, owe and are held to teach faithfully to my said son your said trade of shoemaking. And to provide him decently in health and sickness with food, clothing, and shoes and with all his other necessities throughout all the said time. Promising etc. under the strength [jurisdiction] etc. of the seal etc. I promise and swear etc.

And consequently, I, the said Guillelmus Hospitalis. . . . [Marginal note: by the seal, through faith.][4]

---

[4]The marginal note is opposite a blank space in the register which the notary probably intended to fill in later with the terms agreed to by Guillelmus Hospitalis.

Witnesses: Jacobus Arditi, cultivator, Johannes Ozorii, cleric
of the said place; and I etc.

6. **Apprenticeship Contract**: Folio 56v, dated 14 October 1327:
    In the year and on the day aforesaid, I, Johannes Petri,
furrier of Montpellier, bestow and contract in work and in
study my daughter Cecilia to you, Cecilia, wife of the late
Bernardus Berengarii, grain merchant of Montpellier, present,
namely: from today for four years etc. to work with you and
to do and learn your trade of spinning, hammering, and em-
bossing gold and to do all your other legitimate and honest
biddings for the entire said time. Moreover, you, promising
etc. by reason of the standing agreement between me and you,
ought and are held to teach faithfully to my said daughter
your said trade designated above. And in addition you ought
and are held to give and pay me, receiving for her, 10 *s.t.* in
each year of four years at the feast of the birth of the Lord
[Christmas], and thus I promise etc. For which etc. I obligate
etc. myself and all my present and future property. I renounce
etc. I promise through faith etc.
    And consequently, etc. I, said Cecilia . . . .
[Marginal note: through faith.][5]
    Witnesses: Durantus Belfort, tailor, Guillelmus Michaelis,
gardener of said place, and I etc.

7. **Work Contract**: Folio 68r, dated 31 October 1327:
    In the year and on the day aforesaid, we, both Firminus
de Serviano, goldsmith of Montpellier, and Gaudiosa, spouses,
at the wish and consent of the two of us together and each of
us individually, bestow myself, the said Firminus, in labor and
all my works to you, Johannes Stephani, goldsmith of said
place, present and receiving, namely: for the next two continuous and complete years from today to work with you and

---

[5]The marginal note is opposite a blank space in the register which the
notary probably intended to fill in later with the terms agreed to by Cecilia,
wife of the late Bernardus Berengarii.

to do your trade of goldsmithery throughout the whole said time. And this act having been agreed between us and you, that you will give and will pay to me, the said Firminus, for my labor and salary 10 *s.t.* for each beaten sheet of gold extended to double measure and 20 *s.t.* if by working I extend the same beaten sheet of gold, namely: on the terms customary in the said trade. And we acknowledge and recognize to you as stipulating above that from and in addition to the said salary you will hand over and loan to us 50 *s.t.* that will be repaid to you from the payment of said salary in this manner, namely: 12 *d.* for each beaten sheet of gold that I, the said Firminus, will work and make with you within the said time. Moreover, truly we wish and expressly concede that unless satisfaction is made to you or yours concerning said 50 *s.t.* in the abovesaid manner within the said time that you will be able to seek and demand that which remains to be paid to you of said 50 *s.t.* from us and from our property and from each of us and to have on demand at the wish of you or yours altogether etc. And thus we promise etc. Otherwise etc. Under the strength etc. of the seal etc. we promise and swear etc.

And consequently, etc. I, said Johannes Stephani, etc. promise etc. to you, said Firminus de Serviano, present, etc. that for your said salary I will give and pay 10 *s.t.* for each beaten sheet of gold extended to double measure and 20 *s.t.* if by working you will extend this beaten sheet of gold, namely: according to the said terms customary in the said trade, except 12 *d.t.* which I will retain from your salary for each beaten sheet of gold on account of said 50 *s.t.* to be handed over and loaned by me to you and your said wife as stated above. Otherwise etc. In addition to which etc. For which etc. I obligate etc. myself and all my present and future property. I renounce etc. through faith etc.

Enacted in the royal quarter of Montpellier. Witnesses: Petrus Selvas, resaler, Laurentius Guitardi, grain merchant of Montpellier, and I etc.

This instrument was extracted for the said Johannes Stephani.

8. **Contract for Domestic Service**: Folio 82r–v, dated
    27 November 1327:

    In the year and on the day aforesaid, I, Johannes Raolini
of Pérols, bestow and contract myself as domestic and servant
to you, Galvanus de Cossayveriis, merchant of Milan, present, stipulating and receiving, from today for the next continuous and complete year to stay with you and to do each
and all your legitimate and honest biddings for the entire said
time as much inside the town of Montpellier as outside. Moreover, promising etc., you owe and are held by the express
standing agreement between me and you to provide decently
for me in health and sickness with food, drink, shoes, with a
pair of shirts and a pair of trousers for the entire said time. And
besides you ought to give to me for my salary 30 *s.t.* at the
end of the said year. And I promise etc. Otherwise etc. Under
the strength etc. of the seal etc. I promise and swear etc.

    And wholly, I, Nicholaus Raolini of Pérols, paternal uncle
of the said Johannes Raolini, etc. constitute myself along with
said Johannes etc. surety and principal debtor and guarantor
to you, the said Galvanus, present etc. For which etc. Under
the jurisdiction etc. of the seal etc. I promise and swear etc.

    And subsequently, I, said Galvanus de Cossayveriis, etc.
promise etc. to you, said Johannes Raolini, present, etc. that I
will provide you decently in health and in sickness etc. with
food, drink, shoes, with a pair of shirts and with a pair of
trousers for the entire said time. And besides I will give to
you for your salary 30 *s.t.* at the end of said year. Otherwise
etc. Concerning each and all these abovesaid things promised,
to be considered, and completed by me, I obligate etc. myself
personally and all my present and future property. Under the
jurisdiction etc. of the seal etc. I swear etc.

    Enacted in the royal quarter of Montpellier. Witnesses:
Johannes Panchoni, Bernardus de Henzoto, Bartholomeus
Vitalis of Pérols, and I etc.

    This instrument was extracted for the said Galvanus.

9. **Contract to Provide Shoes**: Folio 86v, dated 4 December 1327:
    In the year and on the day aforesaid, I, Petrus Ricardi, shoemaker of Montpellier, etc. promise and agree with you, Guillelmus Ribas, grain merchant of the said place, present and stipulating and receiving these things for you and for your maidservant Sibienda and for yours, and because of an express standing agreement between me and you whereby I shoe you and your maidservant with good and whole and adequate shoes at my expense, extending for one year from the coming feast of Saint Nicholas etc. And concerning all these completed shoes which will be necessary for you and the same maidservant of yours for going through this town or outside for the entire said year, and I acknowledge etc. that for making the aforesaid you will give and pay to me 24 *s.t.* Concerning which I renounce etc. And thus I promise etc. that in the aforesaid I will not be wanting and I will make these aforesaid well and sufficiently, and I will complete them without controversy. Otherwise, I promise to return etc. all damages etc. Concerning which etc. I obligate etc. myself and all my present and future property. I renounce etc. I promise and swear etc. Under which I promise etc. that my wife will swear to attend to these things along with me at your simple request.
    Enacted in Montpellier. These are the witnesses: Petrus Galterii, cleric, Benedictus Johannis, mercer, inhabitants of Montpellier, and I etc.

10. **Contract to Serve and Sing in a Chapel**: Folio 40r, dated 3 September 1327:
    In the year and on the day aforesaid, I, Guillelmus Ymbaudi, priest of Garrigues in the diocese of Maguelone, bestow and contract myself to you, Johannes Belerude, grain merchant of Montpellier, *procurator*, and in the name of procuration of Brother Henricus de Darbato, *preceptor* of the Teutonic Hospital of Saint-Sauveur of Montpellier, present etc., namely: from the next feast of Saint Luke the Evangelist for the next continuous and complete year to stay in the chapel of the aforesaid

Hospital of Saint-Sauveur and to sing and serve the chantry with one cleric throughout all the said time, in order that it be attended to as is customary in the said chapel. Promising etc. Nevertheless, you in the name of the above procuration or the said *preceptor* or his successor truly ought and will be held to give me for the aforesaid 16 *l.p.t.* in four equal payments within the said year. Moreover, it is agreed and enacted between me and you that all the wine and bread of oblation of the said chapel coming to the altar of the said chapel within the said year are mine. Promising etc. that I will return etc. as expected at the end of said year all things of the church that were given to me etc. Otherwise etc. For which etc. I obligate etc. myself and all my present and future property. I renounce etc. I promise and swear etc.

And completely, we, Raymundus de Mandagoras, chaplain of the church of Sainte-Marie-de-Castelnau of Montpellier, and Petrus Andreas, broker of Montpellier, together and each of them individually certified etc., for the aforesaid, etc. constitute ourselves, along with the said Lord Guillelmus Imbaudi [*sic*] and together as sureties and principal debtors and guarantors to you, said Johannes Belerude as aforesaid *procurator*, present, etc. For which etc. we obligate etc. ourselves together and each of us individually and all our present and future property. We renounce etc. through faith etc.

And consequently, I, said Johannes Belerude as aforesaid *procurator* . . .

[Marginal note: through faith.][6]

Witnesses: Berengarius Baladreg, merchant of Bruges, Clemens Gervasii, scribe of the auction of Montpellier.[7]

---

[6]The marginal note is opposite a blank space in the register which the notary probably intended to fill in later with the terms agreed to by Johannes Belerude, *procurator*.

[7]This is one of the acts where the notary does not include himself among the witnesses.

TRADE

Montpellier was the site of local, regional, and long-distance international trade in the Middle Ages. Commercial transactions took the form of either a recognition of debt with credit involved (*confiteor me debere vobis*), a credit sale (*venditio*), often with a downpayment and a remainder due, or a cash sale (*venditio*). The import trade and local industrial production have left their trace in notarial transactions from a marketplace such as Montpellier. Most transactions of international trade were recognitions of debt with various terms of future repayment included. Silk, wool cloth, linen, spices, and pharmaceutical goods were traded on credit in the Montpellier market and transhipped north to markets in Paris and Champagne; some of these goods also moved northwest to the Atlantic coast and beyond to England, southwest to Spain, and east to the papal court in Avignon. Leather, furs, skins such as rabbit pelts, and wool were part of regional and international trading networks, also based primarily on credit transactions. The transportation industry in animals of transport and burden generally reflected sales on credit. Artisans working in local industry also relied on credit to obtain raw materials. Credit underpinned the wholesale cloth trade, but retail sales in cloth could also be in cash, as they were in the Holanie 1327–28 register. The grain trade touched local, regional, and international commercial spheres, connecting the urban and rural worlds with retail and wholesale transactions in both credit and cash. While many commercial transactions in Montpellier may have escaped drafting by local notaries, a written record of credit transactions reinforced the obligations of repayment.[8] Hence notarial registers record many operations of credit.[9]

Recognitions of Debt

A contract which recognizes a debt that must be paid is rather straightforward. It contains the names of the parties, the debt owed,

---

[8]For a discussion of the role of the notary as an intermediary of trade, see Reyerson, *The Art of the Deal*.

[9]See Reyerson, *Business, Banking and Finance* for a social history of credit in Montpellier.

and the reason for the debt. Debt could be incurred for an endless number of reasons, such as a loan, an unequal exchange of property, a sale, etc. The next several contracts concern recognitions of debt for a variety of items. Even though contracts recognizing debt tend to be rather short, they can be useful in commercial studies, and they are informative with respect to occupations. Recognition of debt contracts might contain a guaranty of repayment by a third party or surety. For a separate surety contract, see Document 25.

11. **Recognition of Debt for a Horse**: Folio 66v, dated 29 October 1327:

In the year and on the day aforesaid, I, Raymundus Bedossii, innkeeper of Montpellier, etc. acknowledge etc. that I owe you, Rostagnus de Duro Forti the younger, cloth merchant of the said place, present etc., namely: 6 *l.* and 10 *s.p.t.* for the price of one horse of dark brown hair with its saddle and its packsaddle etc. I promise to pay etc. on demand etc. upon request etc. Under the jurisdiction etc. of the seal etc. I promise and swear etc.

Enacted in the royal quarter of Montpellier. These are the witnesses: Bernardus de Rocamaura, bleacher, Durantus Ferrerii, cloth finisher of Béziers, and I etc.

The instrument was extracted.

12. **Recognition of Debt for Wool Cloth**: Folios 110v–111r, dated 20 January 1328 (n.s.):

In the year aforesaid and on the twentieth day of the month of January, Lord Charles [reigning] etc., I, Siscle Aurioline,[10] butcher of Montpellier, etc., acknowledge that I owe you, Guillelmus Gasqui, *procurator* etc. of Petrus Teysserii and of Seguinus Baiuli, associated drapers of Montpellier, and to you as notary etc. present etc., namely: 9 *l.p.t.* for the price of wool cloth etc. I promise to pay etc. on demand etc. Under the jurisdiction etc. of the seal etc. I promise and swear etc.

---

[10]The name suggests a woman, though there is no other indication of gender.

Enacted in Montpellier. These are the witnesses: Petrus Oliverii of Teyran, Henricus de Lozena, merchant of Montpellier, and I etc.

13. **Recognition of Debt for Salted Meat**: Folio 24r, dated 8 August 1327:

In the year and on the day aforesaid, we, Petrus Boyssoni, mercer of Montpellier, and Dulcia, spouses, etc. acknowledge etc. that we owe to you, Boninus de Meldeo, merchant, inhabitant of Montpellier, present, etc., namely: 28 *agneaux* of fine gold and of good and just weight for the price of salted meat etc. We promise to pay etc. on demand etc. Under the jurisdiction etc. of the seal etc. We promise and swear etc.

Enacted in the royal quarter of Montpellier. Witnesses: Jacobus Tarnesta, Raymundus Popa, cultivators of the said place, and I etc.

The instrument was extracted.

14. **Recognition of Debt for Beans**: Folio 74v, dated 12 November 1327:

In the above year and on the twelfth day of the month of November, Lord Charles [reigning] etc., we, Petrus Fornerii and Andreas Riberie and Bernardus Riberie and Guillelmus Riberie, all four cultivators of Montpellier, together and each of us individually, etc. acknowledge etc. that we owe to you, Pontius de Gabiano, draper of said place, present etc., namely: 4 *agneaux* of fine gold and of good weight and 4 *s.p.t.* for the price of one quantity of fava beans etc. We promise to pay etc. at the next future feast of the birth of Christ [Christmas] etc. Under the jurisdiction etc. of the seal etc. we promise and swear etc.

Enacted in the royal quarter of Montpellier. These are the witnesses: Raymundus Valesii, grain merchant, Petrus Hugonis, broker of said place, and I etc.

The instrument was extracted.

15. **Recognition of Debt for Silk and Muslin**: Folio 74r,
    dated 11 November 1327:

    In the above year and on the eleventh day of the month
    of November, Lord Charles [reigning] etc., I, Guillelmus Petri
    Amelii of Pomérols in the diocese of Agde etc., acknowledge
    etc. that I owe to you, Petrus del Euze, merchant of Mont-
    pellier, present etc., namely: 60 *agneaux* of fine gold and of
    good weight for the price of cloth of silk and of black muslin
    etc. I promise to pay etc. on demand etc. Under the jurisdic-
    tion etc. of the seal etc. I promise through faith etc.

    Enacted in the royal quarter of Montpellier. These are the
    witnesses: Bernardus Figuerie of Pomérols, Johannes Provinci-
    alis, mercer, Stephanus Bertrandi, button maker of Montpellier,
    and I etc.

    The instrument was extracted.

16. **Recognition of Debt for Byzantine Grain**: Folio 30v,
    dated 14 August 1327:

    In the above year and on the fourteenth day of the month
    of August, Lord Charles [reigning] etc., I, Raymundus Macipi,
    grain merchant of Montpellier etc., acknowledge that I owe
    to you, Petrus Amenlerii, merchant of the said place, legiti-
    mately absent etc., namely: 127 *l.* and 10 *s.* good *p.t.* for the
    price of 300 *sestarii* of grain from Romania etc. I promise to
    pay etc. on demand etc. For which etc. I obligate etc. myself
    personally and all my present and future property. Under the
    jurisdiction etc. of the seal etc. I promise through faith etc.

    Enacted in the royal quarter of Montpellier. These are the
    witnesses: Jacobus Petri, grain merchant, Johannes Peyreneti,
    cultivator of Montpellier, and I etc.

    The instrument was extracted.

Sales

Roman law combined purchase and sale into one contract, *emptio
venditio*. By the thirteenth century, the notarial theorist Salatiele of

Bologna, writing on notarial procedure, separated the two transactions into distinct contracts. In the Holanie acts the difference between a purchase contract (*emptio*) and a sale (*venditio*) was in the wording of the document, with, in the case of a sale, the seller stating he/she was selling and acknowledging the purchase price. In the case of the following acts, movable goods, parts of sheep, fleeces, olive oil, and a book, are involved. *Venditio* of real property will figure in the section on Real Estate and Agriculture. In some cases delivery of the goods sold would be spread over time. In Document 21 grape futures (a form of market speculation) were sold. Sales could be for cash, for a mix of credit and cash, or for full credit.

17. **Sale of Heads and Bellies of Sheep**: Folio 122bis v, dated 4 February 1328:

In the year and on the day aforesaid, I, Johannes Symeonis, butcher of Montpellier etc., sell to you, Bernardus Arneti, cooked-meat seller of Montpellier, present, etc., namely: each and all heads and every and all bellies of each and all sheep and ewes which will be killed by me and in my name and by those partners of mine from the coming feast of the Paschal of the Lord [Easter] up until the next following day of Shrovetide [Lent] for the price, namely: for each dozen of said bellies with the heads of said sheep and ewes 7 *s.* and 6 *d. t.* which you will give and will pay to me for each dozen of those heads with the aforesaid bellies on each Friday which you will have and will receive from me each week, except for 8 *l.t.* which I have had and received from you, concerning and regarding the said aforesaid. In which I renounce etc. Those aforesaid 8 *l.t.* will count for you in the said payment of the price for the said heads with the said bellies from the next future feast of All Saints (1 November) for so long a time retroactively etc. And thus I promise etc. For those etc. I obligate myself personally and all my present and future property. Under the jurisdiction etc. of the seal etc. I promise and swear etc.

And consequently, I, said Bernardus Arneti, etc. agree and promise to you, said Johannes Symeonis, present, etc. and

I agree that for the abovesaid price for each dozen of the said
bellies with the heads of said sheep and ewes I will give and pay
you the said 7 *s.* and 6 *d.t.* which I will give and pay for each
aforesaid dozen of the abovesaid on each Friday concerning
those said heads with the abovesaid bellies which I will have
had and will have received each week except the said 8 *l.t.*
which you had and received from me concerning the aforesaid
prices which ought to be credited to me in the said payment
of the aforesaid prices through the aforesaid means. Otherwise etc. Under the jurisdiction etc. of the seal etc. I promise
and swear etc.

Enacted in the royal quarter of Montpellier. Witnesses:
Raymundus Sicardi, Raymundus Rodesii, cooked-meat sellers
of said place, and I etc.

The instrument was extracted for said B. [Bernardus]
Arneti.

18. **Sale of Fleeces**: Folio 60r, dated 21 October 1327:

In the year and on the day aforesaid, I, Petrus Cortesii,
butcher of Montpellier etc., sell to you, Petrus de Utessia,
bleacher of Montpellier, present etc., each and all of the fleeces
of coarse wool of each and all sheep and of the said coarse
wool [of each and all] ewes which were from the Montagne
Noire and which will be killed by me or in my name from now
until the next future feast of the birth of the Lord [Christ-
mas]. Moreover I make this sale, etc., for 23 *s.t.* as the price
for each dozen which you will give and will pay to me and
mine for each dozen on demand at your first simple request
continuously until you will have had the said fleeces. And thus
I promise etc. Under the jurisdiction etc. of the seal etc.
Through faith etc.

And consequently I, said Petrus de Utessia . . .
[Marginal note: by the seal through faith.][11]

---

[11]The marginal note is opposite a blank space in the register which the
notary probably intended to fill in later with the terms agreed to by Petrus de
Utessia.

Witnesses: Petrus Garini, candlemaker, Johannes Blanchardi, bleacher of the said place.

19. **Sale of Olive Oil**: Folio 67r, dated 29 October 1327:

In the year and on the day aforesaid, we, Petrus de Castriis, beltmaker of Montpellier, and Ermessendis, spouses, and Stephanus Hugonis, weigher of the said place etc., sell to Fulco de Sumena, cleric of the diocese of Nîmes, legitimately absent, etc., namely: 10 *sestarii* of new, sweet, clear, good, beautiful olive oil, not only very marketable but also well bottled according to the standard of Montpellier, for the universal price, namely: 10 *l.* and 10 *s.t.* which we had from him etc. We promise to deliver etc. and to transport etc. to wherever in Montpellier he will wish etc., on demand etc. Under the jurisdiction etc. of the seal etc. We promise and swear etc.

Enacted in the royal quarter of Montpellier. Witnesses: Johannes Fabri, merchant, Petrus Piniani, cultivator of Montpellier, and I etc.

The instrument was extracted.

20. **Sale of a *Codex* (Justinian's *Code*)**: Folios 121v–122r, dated 1 February 1328 (n.s.):

In the above year and on the first day of the month of February, Lord Charles [reigning] etc., I, Anthonius Oliverii, merchant of Majorca, sell publicly in the road etc. to you, master Guillelmus de Sagarra, *jurisperitus* (jurist, a man learned in the law) of Tarrega present, etc., namely: my one *Codex*, covered in green, with the ordinary gloss which begins in the second column of the first page of text "*divi*" and begins in the second column of the said gloss of the said first page "*ad sustentationem*" and begins in the first column of the text of the last folio "*assumpserint*" and begins in the first column of the said gloss of the said last folio "*omnibus maribus.*"[12] Moreover, for

---

[12]The identification of a text written by hand, a manuscript, was often done with a series of first words or first phrases (*incipit*) of the first and last folio page.

this sale, etc. I acknowledge etc. that I had from you etc., in the name of a just and legal price of 20 *l.p.t.* In which I renounce etc. Truly etc. I grant said book to you and yours to have forever etc. Otherwise I promise to return etc. All damages etc. For which etc. and for every eviction etc. I obligate myself and all my present and future property. I renounce etc. I promise by faith etc.

Enacted in Montpellier. These are the witnesses: Petrus Canuti, Bernardus de Hulugia of Tarrega and I etc.

21. **Sale of Grape Futures**: Folio 21v, dated 4 August 1327:

In the year and on the day aforesaid, we, Petrus Mathei and Petrus Andree, both cultivators of Montpellier, etc. sell to you, Guillelmo de Monte Judeo, draper of Montpellier, *procurator*, factor, and business manager usefully on behalf of Petrus Teysserii, draper of Montpellier, and to you, notary etc., namely: all the grapes now hanging in whatever vineyard you hold in rent from Arnaudus Fatis, situated in the *denesium*[13] of Contal bordering the honor of the Hospitallers of the Hospital of Saint-Guilhem. This sale, moreover, etc. according to the weight of Montpellier etc. and for the price which one *saumata* of fruit will be worth generally in Montpellier at the next feast of Saint Gilles (1 September), from which price we had from said Petrus Textoris 6 *l.t.* In which we renounce etc. We make this sale, moreover, etc. under this agreement that said Petrus give and pay to us the remainder of said price at the time of payment for said fruit etc. We promise to deliver etc. and transport etc. at the next harvest at the opportune time etc. Under the jurisdiction etc. of the seal etc. we promise and swear etc.

Enacted in the royal quarter of Montpellier. These are the witnesses: Durantus Lanalh, bookbinder, Petrus de Campis, mercer of said place, and I etc.

---

[13]The term *denesium* refers to land with restricted use.

FINANCE

Notarial registers were the repositories of numerous records of debt of various types, ranging from business and consumption loans to more sophisticated operations of finance including money exchanges, involving the extension of credit in one coinage in one marketplace and the projected recovery of funds in another coinage at another marketplace. Such transactions permitted the movement of funds around Europe. Merchants, artisans, and other notarial clients often had the notary write separate contracts acknowledging the repayment of debt. Acquittals of indebtedness abound in these sources. Debts could be paid through a third party, they could be ceded to a third party, as in Document 26, and guarantors could be formally instituted to stand surety behind debtors, as in Document 25. On occasion, issues of repayment were disputed, as they are today, and the notary would record an arbitration procedure to resolve the controversy (Document 27). The medieval economy was based on credit, the trace of which is found on almost every notarial folio page.

Loans

Loans were generally framed as recognitions of debt. A loan, known as *mutuum* under Roman law, required the actual transfer of something, whether it be goods or money. Generally, as in Document 22, there is no mention of any interest payable for the loan. This was probably due to the fact that the Church considered all interest to be usury, which was prohibited. To avoid an accusation of usury, any interest charged on a loan was written into the amount to be repaid. Any possible profit or interest in the contract below cannot be determined since the value of the thing handed over is not stated. The following loan concerns a woman who had been jailed and was in need of funds for her support and to obtain her release from prison.

22. Recognition of Debt for a Loan (*Causa Mutui*): Folio 88r–v, dated 8 December 1327:
    In the year and on the day aforesaid, I, Guillelma Banassana, daughter of the late Petrus de Banassana of Caveirac in

the diocese of Nîmes etc., acknowledge that I owe you, Laurentius Baudonii, bourgeois of Nîmes, present etc., namely: 25 good *l.p.t.* which I had from you for my necessities described below by reason of a true and legal loan made amicably and graciously to me and received in good money truly counted out and with the real transfer of money taking place, which I set aside, directed toward and spent as much in freeing myself from the royal prison or jail of Montpellier in which I have been detained as for my necessary food while existing in the said jail and also for prosecuting the lawsuit for which I was detained in the said jail. In which I renounce etc. I promise to pay and give back on demand etc. For which etc. I obligate myself and all my property now and in the future. Under the jurisdiction etc. of the seal etc. I promise and I swear etc.

Enacted in Montpellier. These are the witnesses: Jacobus de Bordellis, Johannes Radulphi, merchants of Montpellier, and I etc.

The instrument was extracted.

Money Exchange

A recognition of debt for money exchange (*pro cambio*) was another type of contract, involving the exchange of two different types of coinage. Exchange contracts can be very informative regarding the relationship between coinage and trade as well as credit relationships. Money exchanges were common from the twelfth to the fourteenth century, and they reflected an increasingly complex marketplace where there was access to foreign currencies and where merchants commonly traveled long distances. Money exchange contracts may be read on two levels: 1) as even exchanges in which an amount of one currency was exchanged for an equal value of another coinage; or 2) as exchanges in which profit or interest was built into the exchange so that an amount of one currency was exchanged for a greater or lesser value of another currency. A money exchange contract could provide for repayment in another place, thus allowing merchants to travel without carrying large sums of money. Note that the following exchange contract concerns repayment in money of Valencia in Spain. The term of repayment (*usance*) was twenty days in the case of Valencia; for Barcelona it was fifteen days. The term differed on the basis of the distance from Montpellier.

23. **Recognition of Debt for a Money Exchange (*Pro Cambio*):**
     Folio 18v, dated 31 July 1327:
     In the year and on the day aforesaid, I, Pontius Salati, merchant of Lérida, in my name and in that of Petrus Salati, my brother and partner etc., acknowledge etc. that I owe you, said Guillelmus Romei etc., for you and for Raymundus Hugonis, factor of Petrus Fabri of Montpellier etc., namely: 100 *l.* of royals of Valencia in exchange for other good money, etc. I promise to pay or to have payment made through our factors in the place of Valencia etc., within twenty days etc. I obligate etc. myself and my said brother and partner and all of my property and also his etc. Through faith etc.
     Witnesses: those above.[14]
     The instrument was extracted.

Discharge of Debt and Dispute Resolution

An acknowledgement of satisfaction of debt (acquittal) was drawn up when a debt was paid off or discharged. Generally a notary acknowledged a satisfaction of debt by cancelling his minutes on the contract in the notarial register with the addition of a paragraph of acquittal or by "Xing" out the document. Alternatively, the debtor might require that a separate contract be drawn up upon satisfaction of a debt. The extended form of the debt contract, if it had been drafted, would be destroyed. Provisions for the repayment of debt could involve the establishment of a surety who became responsible for the obligation in the case of the default of the debtor. Indebtedness and accounting could also be handled by transferring of credits to pay off an obligation (cession of rights).

---

[14]Witnesses were the same as those in the preceding act of the Holanie register.

Dispute resolution out of court (*amicabilis compositio*) was a common tactic in the Middle Ages. Lawsuits could be expensive and might drag on for a lengthy period. Often a more efficient and satisfactory restoration of the peace between parties would be a compromise or arbitrated settlement, recorded with some regularity in notarial registers. Disputed debts could be settled in this manner.

24. **Acquittal for Satisfaction of Debt**: Folio 23r, dated
6 August 1327:
    In the year and on the day aforesaid, I, Guillelmus Basselh, mercer of Montpellier, etc. acknowledge etc. to you, Johannes Sizas, of the parish of Saint-Jean-de-Fréjorgues, and Maria, spouses, present etc., that you have satisfied me in each and all debts, notes, credits, and obligations, and in each and all other things in which you, both jointly and individually, and with any other persons, were at any time obligated to me, with charters or without charters, and for whatever reason or cause, up to the present day. Concerning which etc. I make etc. a general acquittal etc. through faith.
    Enacted in Montpellier. These are the witnesses: Guillelmus Holanie the younger, cleric, Hugo Johannis, cultivator of Montpellier, and I etc.
    The instrument was extracted.

25. **Surety for a Debt**: Folios 82v–83r, dated 27 November 1327:
    In the year and on the day aforesaid, I, Macilia, wife of Petrus Corberii, innkeeper of Lattes, present and willing etc., having certified fully as to a debt of 30 *s.* and 8 *d.t.* which only remain in the end thus far to be paid of a larger debt of 60 *s.t.* in which my said husband was obligated to Bernardus Cabrespina, gardener of Montpellier, with the instrument thereupon drafted by Johannes Holanie, royal notary, in the year just above and on the eleventh day of June. Therefore, without making any other change and without other detriment to said instrument and earnestly and in this same [matter], I establish myself along with my said husband and together as

surety and principal debtor and guarantor to you the said Bernardus Cabrespina, present etc., namely: for the said 30 *s.* 8 *d.t.* to be paid by me or mine to you or yours within eight days from next Thursday etc. Under the jurisdiction etc. of the seal etc. and under the oath etc.

Enacted in the royal quarter of Montpellier. Witnesses: Johannes Mathas, second-hand clothes dealer, Petrus de Volio, draper, and I etc.

After this, in the above year and on the tenth day of December, this note was cancelled by the wish of Macilia and Bernardus Cabrespina. Witnesses: Jacobus F . . . de Saulis, salt dealer, Hugo Blanchi, merchant of unfinished wool.

26. **Cession of Rights**: Folio 75r, dated 13 November 1327:

In the year and on the day aforesaid, I, Jacobus de Cabannis, draper of Montpellier etc., cede etc. to you, Jacobus Masselhani, merchant of Montpellier, present etc., namely: all rights and all actions etc. corresponding wholly to me and my demands against and in disagreement with Guillelmus Terasse, late tailor of Montpellier, and against his goods and by reason to wit and on account of one debt of 6 gold *agneaux*. In these 6 gold *agneaux* the said late Guillelmus Terasse was obligated to me . . .[15] by the instrument thereupon drafted by the undersigned notary in the said year of the Lord 1326 and on the third day of the month of September. Concerning which etc., wishing etc. Through faith etc.

After this cession, however, etc. I acknowledge etc. that I had from you etc. 6 *agneaux* of fine gold in which I renounce etc.

Enacted in Montpellier. These are the witnesses: Bernardus Calcadelh, Petrus Basterii, merchant of the said place, and I etc.

The instrument was extracted.

---

[15]Crossed out in manuscript: "under the jurisdiction of the royal seal of Montpellier."

27. Amicable Settlement of Debt (*Amicabilis Compositio*):
Folio 18v, dated 1 August 1327:

In the year and on the day aforesaid, we, Petrus de Salellis of Saint-Paul-de-Montcamel and Alazacia, wife of Jacobus Radulphi of Saint-Pargoire, etc. acknowledge that we owe you, Johanna Egidie, inhabitant of Montpellier, present etc., namely: 40 *s.p.t.* on account of a final reckoning and amicable composition to be made between us and you concerning each and all things that we had to do at any time between us and Mabilia, my, the said Petrus', wife and you, with charters or without charters, and for whatever reason or cause up to this present day, which I, the said Johanna Egidie, acknowledge to be true. In which things, we renounce, etc., promise to pay etc. at the next feast of All Saints etc. Under the jurisdiction etc. of the seal etc. we promise and swear etc.

Enacted in Montpellier. Witnesses: the men [listed] just above.[16]

After this, in the above year and on the tenth day of September, this note was cancelled at the wish of the said Johanna Egidie and Alazacia Radulpha. Witnesses: Lord Raymundus Laurentii, priest, Deodatus Duranti de Torna Mira.

FAMILY

Family ties were very important in the Middle Ages as they were throughout history. Kinship, based on the nuclear family, was embedded in a dense web of ties by blood and marriage, stretching to distant degrees of relatedness. The extended family often had a say in land transactions, as discussed under Real Estate and Agriculture. Notaries were careful to signal family relationships in their contracts. The most significant events in family life, such as marriage, were frequently formalized through contract, as were arrangements for death through estate provisions in last wills and testaments. Gifts could also be made between living persons, often related. Family connections intervened at all levels of life, in business, in real estate, in social relationships.

---

[16]Same as in preceding act of the Holanie register.

Dowry and Marriage

A dowry (*dos*) was the property which a bride and her family gave to the bridegroom as part of a marriage agreement. A contract was necessary to delineate the specific terms regarding the dowry, such as its form and amount, the terms under which the bridegroom acquired the dowry, the terms by which dowry could be transferred to any children of the marriage, or any other terms affecting the dowry. Customarily, in the south of France, the bride legally retained ownership of the dowry, but the bridegroom acquired the right to control, use, profit from, and enjoy the dowry during the marriage, though he was not authorized to dispose of it, at least not without his wife's approval. If, for some reason, the marriage was dissolved or the husband died, the dowry was to be returned to the wife. Other arrangements, however, could be made in the dowry contract. In the contract below, the bride and groom are entering into this agreement in good faith, they are pledging good faith to each other, and they are acknowledging that the marriage will be legal and legitimate. The bridegroom is adding property through an augmentation (*augmentum*) to increase the amount of the dowry.

The medieval practice of giving a dowry in a marriage arrangement was descended from the Roman practice of the same. Dowry practices varied from region to region. The study of dowry contracts reveals such things as the rights of women with respect to property, family and social relationships, and types of property transfers.

28. **Dowry, Marriage, and Augmentation Contract**: Folio 106v, dated 19 January 1328 (n.s.):

In the name of the Lord, amen. In the year of the Incarnation of the Same, 1328 and on the nineteenth day of the month of January, Lord Charles, King of the Franks and Navarre reigning, we, Petrus de la Garriga, of the fortified town of Puéchabon, in the diocese of Maguelone, and Maria, spouses, giving in legitimate matrimony our daughter Bertranda to you, Guillelmus Audemarii, a wine merchant, inhabitant of Montpellier; we give our property, we settle and assign to you, together with our said daughter Bertranda, in dowry, and for a dowry, and in the name of and for the sake of her dowry, namely 20 *l.p.t.* In which and from which you are completely satisfied by us. Whereby I am dowried in the name of Christ, I, the said Bertranda, with the wish, advice and authority of the said Petrus de la Garriga and Maria, spouses, my parents, present, that we, said parents, acknowledge to you, said Bertranda, to be true. I, indeed, the said Bertranda, giving myself in the said legitimate marriage with the said dowry to you, the said Guillelmus Audemarii, and handing myself over to you as your legitimate wife, and receiving you as my legitimate husband, promise and convey to you, receiving, that I will always be good and legal [*sic*] to you and yours, and I will never deceive you or yours in anything. On the contrary, I will always bring you and yours good faith. And thus I receive you in God's and my faith, and I promise to attend to the aforesaid, to serve, to complete, and to oppose or come against you, stipulating, in nothing, through my full and required faith.

And in the aforesaid name of Christ, I, the said Guillelmus Audemarii, through the counsel of my friends, receiving you, the said Bertranda, as my legitimate wife and giving myself to you in legitimate matrimony, acknowledge and recognize that I have had and by counting out have received in good money, counted out, the whole aforesaid dowry from your said parents in entirety. In which I knowingly renounce the claim to have not had and received the counted money and that the entire said dowry was not paid to me. And I give to you, my said wife, from my goods, in augmentation of your aforesaid dowry, three marks of fine silver according to the mark of the town of Montpellier.[17] And also, I constitute and assign you my said wife and to yours through you that entire aforesaid dowry and said augmentation of the dowry in and upon all my present and future goods. For these things I settle the same entire dowry and dotal augmentation on you, my said wife, and on yours to be preserved, given back and restored and at the appropriate time and I arrange in time that

---

[17]Silver and gold of Montpellier were reputed to be of considerable purity.

your said dowry ought to be returned and restored. I obligate myself and all my present and future goods to you, my said wife, stipulating and receiving, for you and yours and yours through you. I renounce therefrom all right, use, and custom by which I might be able to come against the aforesaid or also protect myself. And I agree and promise to you, my said wife, that I will be always be good and above board to you and yours, and indeed, I will never deceive you or yours in anything. I will always bring good faith to you and yours and thus I receive you in God's and my faith. And I promise through my full and required faith to attend, preserve, complete each and every aforesaid thing and in nothing to oppose or come against you, stipulating.

Enacted in Montpellier. These are the witnesses: Bartholomeus Beleti, a bridle maker, and Egidius Arnaudi, a cellarer, inhabitants of Montpellier, and I, Johannes Holanie, etc.

The instrument was extracted for the said Guillelmus Audemarii.

29. **Acquittal for Payment of Nuptial Gift**: Folio 29r, dated 12 August 1327:

In the year and on the day aforesaid, I, Bernardus Huc, wood merchant of Montpellier etc., acknowledge etc. to you, Petrus Huc, wood merchant of the said place, my father, present, etc. that you have paid me fully and entirely those 60 *l.t.* which you gave me on account of a nuptial gift for the sake of the marriage between me and Guillelma, my wife, having contracted concerning the said donation of the said 60 *l.t.* in accord with an instrument thereupon by Johannes de Marginibus, royal notary of Lunel. Concerning which 60 *l.t.* etc. I make etc. a special acquittal etc. I promise and swear etc.

Enacted in Montpellier. These are the witnesses: Stephanus Folcaudi, Petrus Bernardi, mercer, Raymundus de Podio, royal notary, Raymundus Ayere, wood merchant of the said place, and I etc.

Gifts

Medieval inhabitants could choose to make a gift to another person during the lifetime of both (*donatio inter vivos*), as opposed to a testamentary bequest or a gift by the donor with the assumption that he/she would predecease the donee. Such generosity might require a formal act of donation to be recorded by the notary, in which case the gift would be irrevocable.

30. Gift between Living Persons (*Donatio Inter Vivos*):
Folio 116v, dated 26 January 1328 (n.s.):
In the year of the Incarnation of the Lord one thousand three hundred twenty-seven and on the twenty-sixth day of the month of January, and at the hour immediately after terce, with Lord Charles [reigning], etc., I, Johanna, daughter of the late Petrus de Gaps, money changer of Montpellier, with the counsel, wish, authority and express consent of Lady Mirabellis, my mother, wife of my said late father, and Johannes de Pradis and Durantus de Cornhaco, my uncles, and Ladies Johanna Salamone and Ermessendis Cornhage, my aunts, present, which we all the aforenamed Mirabellis, mother, Johannes de Pradis, Durantus de Cornhaco, uncles, Johanna Salamona and Ermessendis Cornhaga, aunts of the said Johanna, assert to be true. I, indeed, the said Johanna, attentive to and considering the many and diverse services and indulgences that you, beloved Stephanus de Albia, my uncle, made and bestowed freely and kindly on me and that you do not cease to make and bestow on me daily, that for much less than the many present donations I hold from you and am not deceived by greater, therefore etc. I give etc., by reason of a pure and simple *donatio inter vivos* etc., to you, the said Stephanus de Albia, my beloved uncle, merchant of Montpellier, present, inasmuch as you merit it, namely, all and each of my goods, mobile and immoble, rural and urban of whatever sort, kind, quantity, and location they be or whether paternal or maternal or by whatever other title or name they are registered or could

be registered that I have today and can and ought to have by reason and authority of whatever mandates and whatever institutions or substitutions and whatever other reason or cause, tacit or expressed, known or unknown up to this present day. I also give in the mode and form etc. all rights and every and all actions, pursuits, petitions and demands etc. pertaining to me and in [my] competence and which I have and can and ought to have in whatever way in the aforesaid goods and by reason and authority of the same aforesaid goods against and in conflict with whatever persons and things, ecclesiastical or secular. Concerning each and all of these aforesaid goods, rights, and actions I utterly divest myself and mine etc. Wishing etc. that etc. I renounce etc. I promise and I swear etc.

Enacted in Montpellier. These are the witnesses: Petrus Benassis, fabricant of combs of Montpellier, Pontius de Bonixanto of Toulouse, and I etc.

The instrument was extracted.

Last Wills and Testaments

The following will and most last wills and testaments offer the historian a gold mine of information on specific individuals, on families, on charity and pious giving, on relationships the testator had with lay people and ecclesiastics, and with family members. Real property and personal effects were often mentioned as part of an estate. When studied in the aggregate, wills offer a window on testamentary behavior of different sectors of the population and on trends in spirituality, both lay and ecclesiastical, as well as insight into the prominence of certain groups such as the friars within medieval religious and certain practices associated with death.

One of the occasions when medieval people of southern Europe had recourse to the notary was to make a will, something they usually did in sickness, in threat of death, in old age, when they were about to undertake long and dangerous journeys, or go on crusade. Pregnant women also made wills, as death in childbirth was very common. In the will of Document 31, on 10 January 1328 (n.s.) Johanna, daughter of merchant Johannes Mercaderii, resident of Montpellier and wife of the jurist Guillelmus Saligani, summoned the notary to her home to have him write her complex last will and testament. Johanna stated that she wanted to arrange her affairs while in good and sane mind and also while she was sound of body. There were other reasons, which become clear in the will, for her proceeding with a last will and testament at this time. Even though Johanna had a son, Johannes, she chose to name her husband as her heir. This may have been the pretext for the will, as her son may have been from a first marriage, often the cause of disharmony in a family. Though there is no explicit evidence, Johanna may have been pregnant with a child by her second husband. Given her tone, she may also have been displeased with her son. At the very least, Johanna wanted to avoid future trouble between him and her husband. In the will she bound her son not to dispute the assignment of her husband as her heir.

Johanna had considerable real property, much of it in the town of Mauguio (Melgueil) and its surroundings, located a few kilometers to the east of Montpellier, and the seat of the county of Melgueil, an old political unit of Lower Languedoc with an important local mint. She herself was probably a native of Mauguio which had continued to represent the center of her interests. She remembered churches and clergy of Mauguio in her pious bequests, as well as friars and churches in Montpellier where she wished to be buried in the cloister of the church of the Dominicans if she died there. She had close associations with the male and female orders of friars, Franciscans and Dominicans, as well as some attachment to the Carmelite and Augustinian houses in Montpellier. The Franciscans, particularly Franciscan women, were important targets of her philanthropy. Johanna arranged for the celebration of masses for her soul and those of her parents and was herself a remarkable exponent of lay charity, bequeathing money for the illumination of many churches, making specific bequests to individual religious, and providing for their clothing and that of orphans through the gift of cloth. Having laid out her wishes regarding her spiritual well-being and her property in great detail, Johanna may have rested more easily when the moment of death was upon her.

This will is produced below as it was drafted in the Holanie register, in a text running many pages. The length of the document and the intricacies of its bequests and dispositions reveal how much care a person might devote to his or her last wishes in the medieval era. The dense web of religious and social connections of the testatrix Johanna suggests that she was the member of a remarkably supportive community and that she was a woman of some affluence.

31. Last Will and Testament:[18] Folios 107r–109v, dated 10 January 1328 (n.s.):

In the name of the Lord, amen. In the year of His incarnation one thousand three hundred twenty-seven and on the tenth day of the month of January, during the reign of Lord Charles, King of the Franks and Navarre, let it be known to all that I, Johanna, daughter of the late Lord Johannes Mercaderii, inhabitant of Montpellier, and wife of Master Guillelmus Saligani, *jurisperitus* and inhabitant of Montpellier, by the grace of God, being of sound body and mind, wanting in my good and sane recollection to dispose of and set in order my goods to provide for the welfare of my soul and of my parents lest later after my death some dispute, question, or controversy may arise concerning these things among my descendants mentioned below or others or anyone; I make my public testament [testament drawn up in the presence of witnesses] as follows: First, I concede my soul to our Lord Jesus Christ and to his mother, the blessed Virgin Mary, and to the Heavenly Court above, and I choose a burial place for my body if death should come to me in Montpellier in the cloister of the church of the Friars Preacher of Montpellier in front of the chapter where I want a certain sepulcher or funeral bed made for me and my said husband and for those of my family who may wish to be buried in the said place if death comes to me in the said place of Montpellier.

Moreover, I do not wish my heir listed below to be held or able to be compelled to have the said sepulcher made. And I take from my goods, for the remedy of my soul and my

---

[18] For the purpose of brevity, non-technical language has been removed and replaced with ellipses. All coin references in this act are to *livres tournois*.

parents and for my funeral, 100 *l.t.* or [that amount] in money
which is circulating on the day of my death. From those 100 *l.*
I leave first to the convent of the Friars Preacher of Montpellier 9 *l.* to be paid as follows below, and I ask the said friars
that they celebrate masses for my soul and for the souls of my
lord parents, as many for the dead as for the Holy Spirit, and
that for each obituary mass my heir mentioned below will pay
from the said 9 *l.t.* to the prior of the said order 30 *s.* And that
he ought to have and pay for six obituary masses within one
year at the longest after my death.

Likewise, I leave to the convent of the Friars Minor of
Montpellier 40 *s.* of the said money and I ask the said
brothers that two be obliged to celebrate as many [masses] for
the dead as for the Holy Spirit for my soul and for the souls
of my parents and that for each obituary mass my heir listed
below ought to pay from said 40 *s.* to the guardian of the said
order 20 *s.* within a year of my death. . . . I leave to the convent[s] of Carmelite friars and Augustinian friars of Montpellier, to each convent, 20 *s.*, and I ask the friars of the said
orders that on the day the said 20 *s.* are paid to them they
celebrate masses for the dead and make special commemo-
rations for my soul and for the souls of my parents. . . . I leave
to the convent of those of Prouilhan and to the convent of the
Sisters Minor of Montpellier, to each convent, 10 *s.*, and I ask
the said religious ladies that they hold me and my family in
their prayers in community. . . . I wish and I order moreover
that in the *castrum* of Melgueil in the church of Saint-Jacques
ten priests of the parish from the *castrum* of Melgueil chant
three funeral masses . . . .[19] And I ask the said lord priests that
through the said masses at the end of these funeral masses that
each one of them according to their usual custom ought to
pray at the sepulcher where my lord father lies. And I leave to
each of these said lord priests 6 *d.* and I want the three aforesaid funeral masses to be sung within a year of my death. . . . I

---

[19]Melgueil is the medieval name for the modern Mauguio, a town several
kilometers from Montpellier.

leave 2 *s.* to the chaplain, curate of the church of Saint-Denis of Montpellier, and 6 *d.* to the deacon of this same church if death comes to me in Montpellier, otherwise nothing. . . . I leave to all the priests who marched in company with my remains to the grave, to each 5 *d.* . . . I leave for the lights of Notre-Dame-des-Tables and Al Resenh and of Saint-Denis of Montpellier 12 *d.*, so much once and for all. . . . I leave 5 *s.* for my end to the charity of the confraternity of Sainte-Katherine of Melgueil, and that the provost of the said confraternity be obliged to sing one obituary mass for my soul as is customary. . . . I leave for the lights of Saint-Jacques of Melgueil, of Notre-Dame, of Saint-Pierre, of Saint-Blaise, of Sainte-Katherine, of Sainte-Magdalene, of Saint-Michael, and concerning the hosts and torches of Saint-Jacques with which the body of Christ is raised and for the candle that burns night and day before the altar of Saint-Jacques of Melgueil, to each 6 *d.* . . . I leave 3 *d.* for each of the lights of the church of Notre-Dame of Melgueil. Likewise, I leave 4 *d.* for the torches. . . . I leave 3 *d.* for the lights of the Saint-Esprit of Montpellier. . . . I leave 3 *d.* for the candle which burns there night and day. . . . I leave 4 *d.* for the lights of Sainte-Croix of Melgueil. . . . I leave for the lights of Sainte-Christine, Saint-André, Saint-Martin, and Saint-Thomas near Melgueil, to each 3 *d.* . . . I leave 10 *s.* to all ladies who mourn the souls in purgatory in Montpellier so . . . that many people may mourn. . . . I leave 10 *s.* at most to the ladies who collect for the food of the poor lying in the hospitals of Montpellier. . . . I leave to the hospital of orphans of Montpellier one cord of linen from which I wish my heir to have shirts made for the little orphans of said hospital. . . . I leave 5 *s.* for captives to be redeemed.[20] . . . I leave 10 *s.* to Alazacia, *ancilla* of Lady Carnassa. . . . I leave 10 *s.* to Floreta who lives with the said Lady Carnassa. . . . I leave 20 *s.* to Guillelmeta Blancharde of Aniane, once my servant. . . . I leave 10 *s.* to Friar Petrus Nicholai,

---

[20]The Charity of the Redemption of Captives refers to those captured and enslaved by infidels, mostly in the Mediterranean world.

partner of Friar Johannes Mercaderii, my nephew, of the Order
of Preachers. . . . I leave 10 *s.* to Friar Johannes Catalani of
the Order of Augustinians of Montpellier. . . . I leave 10 *s.* to
Friar Stephanus de Sumidrio of the same order. . . . I leave
20 *s.* to Friar Bertrandus Agulhoni of the order of Friars Minor
of Montpellier from those 30 *l.* which Johannes Agulhoni, his
brother, owes to me. . . . I leave 10 *s.* to Johanna, daughter of
Johannes Macipi of Melgueil. . . . I want three cords of linen,
up to the quantity worth 30 *s.* among the three, to be made
into shirts and to be given to the begging poor within the
castrum of Melgueil within a year of my death. . . . I leave 100 *s.*
to Guiraudus Johannini, my cousin. . . . I leave 100 *s.* to
Marita, wife of Master Raymundus Mameti. Likewise, I leave
100 *s.* to Tibos, daughter of Guillelmus Coq of Lodève, my
brother, born of the same mother. Likewise, I leave 100 *s.* to
Perrotus, nephew of the said Marita, to be paid according to
the wishes of my said husband. Likewise, I leave 100 *s.* to Lord
Bernardus Bone, priest, my cousin. . . . I leave to Guillelmus
and Jacobus Bone, brothers, my cousins, 50 *s.* each. Likewise,
I leave 50 *s.* to Francisco Gifre, my cousin. And I do not wish
that, from this time forth, they be able to lay claim to anything in my goods or in the inheritance from my late lord
father. On the contrary, I wish that before my below-listed
heir pay anything to the publicly declared Lord Bernardus
Bone, Guillelmus and Jacobus Bone, and Franciscus Giffre
[*sic*] from the said legacies that they be held to make full
acquittal and release to my said heir concerning all they can
seek generally in my inheritance and that of my said late
father and also a perpetual pact, personal and real. Likewise, I
leave 20 *s.* to Lord Jacobus Carrayroni, priest. . . . I leave 10 *s.*
to Ermessendis, daughter of Petrus Alvernhas of Melgueil. . . .
I leave 10 *s.* to Bonassies, daughter of Imbertus Fangatore. . . .
I leave 10 *s.* to Petronilla, wife of the late Petrus lo Cort. . . . I
leave 10 *s.* to Beatrix, wife of the late Petrus Berengarii. . . . I
leave 10 *s.* to the widow Pascala, who lives next to the Friars
Minor of Montpellier. . . . I leave 10 *s.* to Vierna, daughter of

the late *Dena*[21] Baias of Melgueil. . . . I leave 100 *s.* to Guillelmeta, daughter of Bernardus Salorardi of Sommières. . . . I
leave 100 *s.* to Pontius Nigri, my cousin of Lunel. . . . I leave
50 *s.* to Gaudiosa, my cousin, wife of Johannes Bedelli. . . . I
leave to Lord Bernardus Bone for his lifetime, and that is all,
the usufruct of that small house of mine which adjoins on one
side the house of the late *Den* Bona Sorient and on the other
side with the *palherium* of my house, and on another side with
another part of the said house of mine which was customarily
rented out and with the street that looks at the crossroads of
Lady Meravelle. And I wish that after the death of the said
Lord Bernardus it revert to my heir listed below or to his
heirs. Likewise, I leave from my goods every year to the convent of the aforesaid Friars Preacher of Montpellier an additional 20 *s.* in current money, owing rent, without counsel or
eminent domain which I wish to have paid to the said convent every year on the day when death came to me, except the
first year of my death. And I ask the said friars who are now
and will be [there] in the future that on that day on which the
said 20 *s.* are paid to them or to the prior of the said order
they ought to celebrate [a mass] for the dead for the redemption of my soul and for my sins and those of my husband and
of my parents. And I wish and order that if my heir listed
below or his successors wish to reclaim the said 20 *s.*, owing
rent, upon another possession inside the jurisdiction of Montpellier, that he be able to do this and to assign the said 20 *s.*
to the said convent. And, having done this, that my said heir
and all things inherited from me may be free from all obligation in which they may be found by the strict law to the said
convent and also from the guaranty and payment of the said
20 *s.* Likewise, I leave to my beloved nephew, Friar Johannes
Mercaderii of the order of Friars Preacher every year that he
will live among men 60 *s.* in current money which I wish to
be paid to him at the feast of the birth of the Lord [Christ-
mas] except the first year after my death because I made many

---

[21] *Dena* or *Ena* meaning Lady; *Den* or *En* meaning Sir.

other legacies above. And I wish that with the death of said
Friar Johannes the said 60 *s.* be held to return to my heir listed
below and his heirs and that nothing can be sought for the
order of the said Friars Preacher by reason of the said 60 *s.*
from my said heir below or his [heirs]. Likewise, even more I
accept for my soul and for the souls of my parents and of my
said husband and all of my family every year in perpetuity two
sestaria of grain such that two parts are wheat and the third
barley, which two *sestaria* I want to be given through my heir
listed below and through the future possessors by whatever
means or whatever title, the major part which is in the allod
of my paternal house in Melgueil which is in front of the
hospital of the poor; these two *sestaria* I want given always and
perpetually every year in baked bread to the mendicant poor
in the *castrum* of Melgueil. And this for eight days before the
festival of the birth of the Lord. Likewise, I obligate and I
wish to remain obligated such part of my said house that is in
free allod and this perpetually for the said two *sestaria* as stated
above be paid every year and expended for the love of God.
And also for the said 60 *s.* to be paid to Friar Johannes Mercaderii each year as long as he will live among men. Likewise,
I leave to the hospital of the poor of Melgueil one bed sup-
plied with bed clothes. . . . I leave according to the law of institution [of heirs] to Johannes, my son, that land of mine with
its obligations that I hold in the place called Cumbas de Carin-
han, next to the *mansus* of the said Den Rogier which is
fronted from one side with the honor of the so-called Raymundus de Conchis of Montpellier, with the street in between,
and on two sides with the honor of Johannes de Rodesio,
changer of Montpellier, which land I want the said Johannes,
my son, to have after my death if and when he accomplishes
with effect each and every condition written below, and when
he does and completes all the things below to be ordered by
me, and otherwise not. . . . I leave to my said son according to
the law of the institution [of heirs] after death of my heir below
another land which I hold next to the church of Saint-André

which is fronted on one side by the honor of Johannes Andree and on another side with the honor of Martinus Stephani, and on another side with the public street which goes from Saint-André to Sainte-Christine which is held in part by the lord bishop of Maguelone and with his consent. . . . I leave to my said son by the law of the institution [of heirs] after death of my said heir below certain other of my land which is situated next to the route to Lunel in the *decimaria* of the church of Saint-Aunès-d'Auroux²² and is fronted on one side with the route from Lunel, and on another side with the stream called Valauria, and on another side with the vineyard of Master Guiraudus Magistri, physician. . . . I also leave to my said son by the law of the institution [of heirs] that vineyard of mine which is next to the road to Montpellier, and in that *decimaria* and fronted on one side with the honor of the heir of the late Johannes Moneti, and on another with the honor of the heirs of Petrus Droc. And it is held by the lord bishop of Maguelone. . . . I also leave to my said son a certain other vineyard of mine located in the tenement of Malsanc in the *decimaria* of the church of Notre-Dame of Melgueil and fronted on one side with the honor of Petrus Juliani and on another with the honor of Franciscus Giffre [*sic*], and on another with the honor of the late Petrus Plantas. And I wish [my said son] to hold and possess the aforesaid possessions except the first one given to my heir below as a dotal holding for his entire life. And I wish and order that my said son be content with the aforesaid goods of mine in this manner that he be able to seek nothing more in my said goods by whatever reason or cause. Being sound, I wish and order that all revenues or fruits which were hanging [on the vine] or in whatever way will ripen during the entire year in which death comes to my heir; regarding the said possessions willed to my aforesaid son, by the law of the institution [of heirs], they are and ought to belong to my heir listed below. And that my said heir be strong concerning the said fruit and produce and willingly dispose of

---

²²In Latin, *Beata Maria de Ozorio.*

and order at his pleasure. Likewise, I wish and order that if
my said son makes some issue or controversy in justice or
outside by word or by deed against my heir below by reason of
the aforesaid inheritance or by whatever other means by these
events, in that case all the aforesaid goods above left by me to
him by the law of institution [of heirs] I take away and
remove and I wish him to be held for no legacies. And in this
event I wish him to be content with 30 *l.* of current money
which I leave him according to the present law of institution.
And that he can seek nothing more by another reason or
cause in relation to my goods, and I wish the aforesaid things
left by me above to pertain to my same heir below by the law
of inheritance. . . . I wish and order that if my said son wants
to enjoy the aforesaid things left by me above through the law
of institution or any other thing from these, I wish that before
all he made a liberation and full acquittal with a public instrument to my heir below concerning all law and action which
he has or he is able to have in whatever manner in all my
aforesaid property and in my estate by whatever reason or
cause, and also that he make perpetual agreement, personal
and real, with my said heir of not seeking anything in my
whole estate by himself or another in any way. That also if he
does not wish to make or mount some question or controversy in law or outside against my heir by reason of the said
inheritance or on account of the below mentioned goods to
mount some complaint by laws to sell through me after the
death of my heir by these pretexts and in whatever of them or
even if my said son contests the present will in anything, I
wish my said son to be content with the said 30 *l.* Likewise, I
wish and order that all my possessions listed below be sold after
the death of my heir listed below and publicly distributed at
auction, and I wish the price or prices of the said things to be
given or allocated in pious causes for my soul and for the
souls of my parents and of my said husband and all my family.
In like manner that a third part of the price of my things
written below be allocated for the celebrating of masses as

much in Montpellier in the church of the Preachers as in Melgueil in the church of Saint-Jacques. Also indeed, a third part be placed as much in wool cloth for winter as in linen for summer to be allocated to the mendicant poor of Christ and to the disgraced who nevertheless may be greatly in need. Indeed, another third part be allocated for the love of God for the food and for the restoration of the poor in the hospitals or parishes of Montpellier and Melgueil, in promised food for the poor lying there ill to be made or administered in such way. I wish the virtuous ladies or matrons of Montpellier to be called who are charged to be dispatched for these promises by my executors listed below and for these things that this be fulfilled through them explicitly. Indeed, I pronounce that those possessions which I wish to have sold after the death of my said heir listed below are these. First, a certain vineyard and some land attached nearby which are in the *decimaria* of the church of the Saint-Aunès-d'Auroux in a place called Al Castanhier and which is fronted on one part with the honor of Guillelmus Chanpanhas and with the possession of Pontius Deodati, moneyer, and with the possession of Pontius Vitalis. . . . A certain other vineyard of mine which is held by Armandus de Valhanquesio, containing three *carteriate*[23] or thereabouts, situated in the *decimaria* of the church of Notre-Dame of Melgueil next to the wood of the lord bishop of Maguelone which is fronted on one part with the honor of Pontius Thome, and on another with the honor of Petrus de Roca Forcada of Melgueil, and another with the wood of the said lord bishop. . . . My other land containing nine *sestariate*[24] or thereabouts which is next to Saint-Martin-de-Canayraco and is held from the lord of Candillargues for the yearly *census* of 2 *s.t.* and it is fronted with the honor of Berengarius de Texerio on one part and on another with the honor of the children of the late Petrus Hugonis of Melgueil and on another part with the river called *Cadola* (Cadoule), and likewise, my

---

[23]The dipthong collapses.
[24]The dipthong collapses.

threshing-floor which is in the said tenement at Petra Fixa[25] in the *decimaria* of the church of the Notre-Dame of Melgueil and is fronted on one part with the honor of Guillelmus Vesiani with the cart path in between, and on another part with the threshing *area* of Raymundus Juliani and with the possession of Durantus Ohieu. . . . Two pieces of land, one of which contains in it two *sestariate* and an *eyminata*, the other one *sestariata*, which are in the said tenement [of] Clamiapeyra in the *decimaria* of the church of Saint-Jacques of Melgueil, which is fronted on one side with the honor of Raymundus Pascalis, and on another with the honor of Guillelmus Vesiani. . . . Another piece of land is fronted on one part with the honor of the heirs of the late Petrus Droc, and on another with the honor of him who is called Galnauh, a cultivator. . . . One meadow of mine which is in the meadow of Candillargues which is fronted with the possession of Egidius Garinii, and with the possession of Johannes Junini. . . . One meadow of mine situated in the *decimaria* of the church of Saint-Barthélémy of Aleyrargues and fronted on one side with the honor of the hospital of the poor of Melgueil and on the other with the honor of Johannes Serinhani of the said place. And it is in free allod. . . . A certain wood which is in the place called Romeyra on the cart or carriage road along the road which leads from Melgueil toward Montpellier, and it is fronted on one part with the honor of Johannes Renouerii and has the ingress through the said honor of the said Johannes Renouerii, and on another part with the wood of Saint-Esprit of Montpellier, and on another part with the honor of Johannes Pauleti, wood merchant of Montpellier. . . . One garden of mine which is held from the church of Saint-Jacques and is in the garden of Petra Fixa and is fronted on two sides with public roads, and on another with the garden of the wife of Pontius Bedelh, and on another with the garden of Guillelmus Veziani. . . .

---

[25]Perhaps a place-name for a physical outcropping or an erected or fixed stone.

My vineyard situated at Crosos[26] which is in free allod and is
fronted with the possession of Thomas Gavaudani and Raymundus Gavaudani and with the road which leads from
Melgueil to the mill [of] Den Blanquier. And I wish and I
order that at the time when the abovesaid vineyard is sold, two
sestarii of wheat be imposed and assigned without perpetual
revenue domain, to be given in cooked bread for the love of
God after the death of my heir listed below with another two
sestarii of grain bequeathed by me and which will be given at
the said time in which the other two *sestarii* ought to be given
and in the said place of Melgueil to the poor mendicants there.
And I wish that in that year in which death comes to my said
heir, my said heir be able to order and dispose according to
his wishes concerning the revenues of the said possessions and
to hold and peacefully and quietly possess the said possessions
during the whole time of his life. I, in good health, wish and
order that concerning my possessions designated and situated
just above, they can and ought to be sold in entirety after my
death with the knowledge of my said heir and of Friar Johannes
Mercaderii up to the quantity of 100 *l.t.* with which he may
satisfy regarding all the above legacies made by me as much
pious [legacies] as others, and concerning the following expenses. And because they may obligate other of my aforesaid
property by eviction, I make my husband and the said brother
Johannes Mercaderii executors, as much to execute the promises and pay the legacies. And I wish and order that the
aforesaid possessions which remain, as located above, be sold
after the death of my heir listed below by the religious and
the prior of Saint-Jacques of Melgueil who now is or will be
at the time and through Friar Johannes Mercaderii, my aforesaid nephew if he survived. If, however, he did not survive, in
that case, I wish that whoever will be prior of the Preachers
convent at that time, along with the said lord prior of Saint-
Jacques will sell and ought to sell the said possessions freely,
without obstruction, and dispose of and spend the price of

---

[26] A place name meaning pit.

these things for pious causes as it is stated above at the risk of their souls. And I wish and order that the aforesaid Friar Johannes and my heir listed below not be compelled through some judge at the instance of some one of the aforesaid legatees to pay out some legacies made to them within a year of my death unless some from the aforesaid possessions should be sold up to the sum of the aforesaid legacies concerning which he can be satisfied. I wish, moreover, that said Friar Johannes and my heir ought to make and arrange with effect that all the aforesaid pious legacies be paid out within a year of my death from the price of the possessions to be sold by them, as it is stated above. And I do not want that before the end of the year they may be compelled by anyone to have this done. Likewise, I wish and order that from the remainder of said 100 *l.*, if there is one, that my aforesaid heir and the aforesaid Friar Johannes cause to be made a strong sepulcher or monument, which was mentioned above, in which I and my said heir and those of my family, who will want to lie there, may be buried. And this moreover, if death comes to me in Montpellier. Indeed, in all my other property, mobile and immobile, rights, and whatever actions, I institute my beloved husband Master Guillelmus Saligani as my universal heir, in his own name.

This is my last will and testament which I praise, approve, champion, ratify, and confirm, and I wish to be valid in all ways. Breaking, interrupting, annulling that will of mine made by me formerly by the hand of Master Bernardus Catalani, notary of Melgueil, in which were words of repeal such that I could make another will with the passage of time. I wish, direct and order that it have no strength unless these repeal words are placed expressly from word to word; namely, that I wrote, I wrote [*sic*] Jesus of Nazarus, King of the Jews, entitled triumphant, have pity on us. Breaking also all other testaments, codicils, and last wills, formerly made by me or made in whatever way, by this present testament in its strength, perpetually valid, and if it happens that it not be suitable that this present testament remain valid by testamentary law, I wish and order that it be valid by the law of codicils or by that of some other law of last will. I wish and order that if it happens that I make another will that it have no strength unless mention be made expressly of these words in that will which words are such. Possessing the property of others, let him have no just cause for not holding [it] unless it is understood by his intention to restore [it] in entirety. And I ask that you, the two undersigned witnesses, when the occasion will appear concerning the aforesaid, you present witness (testimony) of the truth.

This present testament was enacted and made by the said testatrix in Montpellier, in the house of the same resident and of her husband, in a certain room of said house. And these witnesses were called by the said testatrix and specially to speak to these things: the aforesaid friars, Friar Johannes Mercaderii, Friar Petrus Nicholai, brothers of the Order of Friars Preacher, Masters Egidius Johannis, Phillipus Ganterii, Jacobus Perayroni, royal notaries, Matheus Pargamenerii, Ferrandus Escalardi, furrier of Montpellier, and I, Johannes Holanie, royal public notary who, having been asked, requested, and ordered by the said testatrix, drew up all and every thing in this document.

The instrument was extracted.

REAL ESTATE AND AGRICULTURE

Land represented a major source of wealth in the Middle Ages. It was also the major source of prestige and power. The agricultural economy sustained many types of economic operations, and the vast majority of the medieval population lived on the land, not in towns. Real estate transactions were among the earliest ones committed to writing in the Middle Ages. Family interests in land ran deep, and sale or alienation of land usually required the approval of family members, as illustrated in Document 34. The importance of land was felt as strongly in towns as it was in the countryside. Merchants and other townspeople were anxious to acquire land as investments and for the status its possession conveyed. Agricultural occupations were common among townspeople who engaged in small-scale commercial farming, vineyard cultivation, and the production of grain. There were a whole host of contracts associated with real estate and agriculture of which a sampling are provided below.

Sales

The land sales contract took the form of *venditio* in which seller and buyer agreed to what was to be sold, the terms of sale, and the price involved. (See earlier discussion.) In the following document, one of the few unabbreviated acts in the Holanie register, and thus rather lengthy, the seller Stephanus Sospontis, junior, a gardener of Montpellier, and his wife Guillelma, sold a garden and four adjoining houses in a suburb of Montpellier near the house of the Templars which had become the Order of St. John of Jerusalem (the Hospitallers), to Bernardus Egidii, also a gardener of Montpellier, for a price of 40 *l.p.t.* This property was under the eminent domain (*dominium directum*) of Rigaudus de Broa, merchant of Montpellier, who received an annual revenue of 6 *l.p.t.* and approval rights to the transfer of the property for which he was paid 4 *l.p.t.* Note that the property is described by its relationship to neighboring properties. This type of property description predates the metes and bounds legal descriptions which are often used today. The full text version of this sale provides students with exposure to the legal formulas which peppered notarial acts and which were hidden by abbreviations in most of the acts of this book. On the basis of full texts it is possible for the historian to reconstruct abbreviated texts in a fashion not dissimilar to that used by the medieval notary when he pro-duced an extended copy of the contract for his clients.

32. **Sale of Land and Houses (*Venditio*):** Folios 1r–2v, dated
    7 July 1327:
        In the year of the Incarnation of the Lord 1327 and on
    the seventh day of the month of July, Lord Charles, King of
    the Franks and Navarre reigning, we, Stephanus Sospontis the

younger, gardener of Montpellier, son of the late Stephanus
Sospontis, gardener of said place, and of Johanna, his late
wife, and Guillelma, wife of the same Stephanus Sospontis,
namely: I, said Guillelma at the wish, counsel, authority, license,
and express assent and consent of said Stephanus Sospontis,
my husband, present, that I, said Stephanus Sospontis, husband of the same Guillelma, acknowledge to be true; indeed
we both, said Stephanus Sospontis and Guillelma, spouses,
having been made principal sellers of the things written below,
together and each of us individually, for us and our successors
and heirs of law and fact, universally and singly, in good faith
and good conscience, with all deceit and fraud removed completely and exclusively with this true and public instrument now
and in perpetuity, firmly and validly we sell, give, cede, and
concede and hand over with a clear, perfect and irrevocable
but always valid title of sale, we transfer as if and in perpetuity
we abandon to you Bernardus Egidii, gardener of Montpellier,
present, buying, stipulating solemnly and receiving on behalf
of you and your successors, according to all the wishes of you
and of your successors in life and in death, perpetually and fully,
to be carried out, giving, selling, changing, mortgaging or
alienating in whatever way you or yours will wish, to whatever
persons except to holy clerics and *milites*, moreover, with counsel,
always direct domain and approval and the right of first approval of Rigaudus de Broa, merchant of Montpellier, and his
successsors and the *census* or *usaticum* of 6 *l.p.t.* to the same
Rigaudus de Broa and his successors to be paid each year at
the Paschal Feast of the Lord [Easter], namely: one whole garden of ours with four houses contiguous to the same garden,
of which four houses three are attached contiguous and with
the third part of a well which is next to the said garden in the
garden of another Stephanus Sospontis and with all ingress,
egress, and other appurtenances and its rights, situated in the
suburbs of the town of Montpellier behind the house and church
of the former Temple, now of the Order of Saint John of
Jerusalem, and bordering on one side with the kitchen garden

of said house of the former Temple, with the public road in the middle, and on the other side with the garden of the said other Stephanus Sospontis,[27] gardener, and on the other side with the garden of Bertrandus Caponi, gardener, and on the other side with the garden of Johannes Menatoris, pepperer, with the town wall in the middle.

Moreover, for this sale, cession, and concession of the aforefronted garden and of the said four houses contiguous with the said third part of a well and with all their appurtenances and rights, we acknowledge in truth and from certain knowledge we recognize that we have had from you and, having reckoned, have received in good money, counted out in the name of a just and legal price, 40 *l.* of good *p.t.* which aforesaid price we assert to be ample, good, competent and just. Concerning which we hold ourselves well placated by you and content. And in the aforesaid things with certain knowledge, we renounce a claim that the money had not been counted out and not received and that the total aforesaid price had not been had and had also not been paid. Truly, if the aforefronted garden with the said four houses, contiguous with each other and with the said third part of the said well and also with all their appurtenances and rights is worth more than the above stated price now or will be or will be able to be in the future, all that plus whatever is or should be also affecting [it] if it exceeds more than half of the just price, we will give [it] to you the said buyer as well worthy and to yours through you under the said price, and we will give [it] in good spirit by a pure and simple donation among the living with no cause for ingratitude or penitence or whatever other else, revoking [it] in the future.

Concerning which aforefronted garden and four houses contiguous with the same garden and with the third part of the said well and also with all other rights of property and possession and all else which we have in them or ought to have or are seen to have or have had at any time together or apart

---

[27] Homonyms were quite common in a town the size of Montpellier.

for whatever reason or cause, and I, Guillelma, by reason and action of my dowry, my *hypotheca*, or my dotal augmentation or for whatever other reason, divest ourselves and those of ours absolutely and we invest you and yours completely concerning these things, and we transfer and also transport to you and yours.

And indeed we make and constitute you *procurator* for your right and just possession and concerning your own and for your legitimate purchase, inasmuch as the best and useful authority to be said, dictated, written, or considered can or will be prudent for your circumstance and for your uses. Moreover, we hand over to you, receiving, this aforefronted garden and said four houses contiguous with this garden and with the aforesaid third part of the said well and all its rights and its appurtenances or as it were we hand over completely and we relinquish forever the stripped and vacant possession. And as an indication of said transfer of possession or, as it were, and having transferred *usaticum* to the lord we manually hand over the instruments for the aforefronted garden and for the said four houses contiguous with it and with the third part of the said pertinent well, by which transfer of instruments we wish, understand, and judge you to be present and receiving and introduced into the bodily possession, as it were, of this aforefronted garden and the said four houses contiguous with it and with the said third part of the aforesaid well and of all its rights and its appurtenances, willing and conceding to you as above stipulating, and to yours, for your sake that you and your men, by your own authority, that you did not ask for our vacating but being in complete ignorance of such things and having expected no other authority you may be able and it may be valid, whenever it may have pleased you or yours to have entered, to take hold and obtain physical possession, as it were, of this aforefronted garden and of said four houses contiguous with this garden and with the said third part of the aforesaid well and of all its rights adjoining or appurtaining to it. And since until you will take physical possession of all of the aforesaid you will be uneasy about us, the sellers, towards you, we established possession to be held in your name and that of your men in the meantime.

We add and assert that the aforefronted garden with said four houses contiguous with it and with the said third part of the well and with all its appurtenances and rights are for you and yours to observe full jurisdiction, not just civil or natural, within our possession or another of us or our men, to some extent remaining, ceding, and ordering us as above; we stipulate for you and yours every thing and all rights, all actions, petitions, pursuits, calls, causes and demands, real and personal, ordinary and extraordinary, mixed, main, civil, expedient, and direct, principal, and accessory, and things pursued and others which in whatever way and by whatever name were kept safe for us, coinciding and meeting on occasion and by intuition, of the aforefronted garden and said four houses contiguous with it and the aforesaid third part of the aforesaid well and all its rights and its appurtenances against and adverse to whatever persons and things ecclesiastical or secular.

And we promise, together and each of us individually, and we convey to you said buyer, stipulating as above to your men and for you, that we and whoever of our men and our successors, make over to you and your successors and those whom you wish all of the aforefronted garden with said four buildings contiguous with it and with the said third part of the aforesaid well and with all its rights of ingress and egress, appurtenances, and rights always to have, to hold, continually, peacefully, and quietly, to possess all this, the entire garden aforefronted with the said four buildings contiguous with it and with all of the third part of the aforesaid well and with all other appurtenances and its rights to you and your successors. We defend, preferring and protecting ourselves in court and outside of court, with our costs and expenses against or adverse to whatever persons in the aforefronted garden and in the said four buildings and the third part of the said well, are making petitions, questions, suits, or other demands.

Thus we promise and convey to you, as stipulating above, that whoever of our *procurators*, every and each person having in whatever way and from whatever cause, right, and actions in the aforesaid garden and four buildings and a third part of the said well, they will praise and confirm the present sale and every and each of the things written above, with our own costs and expenses from day to day at the every wish of you and yours and at the first simple request and summons which holds for a certain term. Otherwise we promise to return and correct any damages, injury, interest, and expenses and costs for you and yours if it happens that these are incurred or suffered for the aforesaid or others of the aforesaid by you and yours. Concerning the above we wish to believe [you] on your simple word or that of yours alone without oath, witnesses or any other type of proof. For every and all of the aforesaid to be considered and completed and for every and all eviction in the said aforefronted garden and in the said four houses and the third part of the said well or one of those or of their parts be lumped together or in part to you said buyer and your successors, we obligate ourselves and our successors to give back and restore in full to you and your successors.

We submit to you as above stipulating and through you to yours out of certain knowledge ourselves in person alone and each of us together and all our present and future goods, of each of us together, under the strength of the district and power of the seal of Montpellier of the king of the Franks and Navarre in the sway and jurisdiction and on pain of imprisonment of the court of the said seal, for us and our goods to be placed under [it], renouncing thenceforward concerning these things knowingly and expressly, certified in fact and consulted in law fully and informed in law and having made an exception of the ignorance of fraud and graft and of the action in fact and with these rights articulated any other deception which may be made in another contract of sale beyond half the just price which will be given to you by contract or will supplement the just price and through pact with those privileges and royal statutes and rights through which, losing their goods, they will be freed from prison by privilege of the cross, or the jurisdiction of the letter of the Emperor Hadrian[28] in the new constitutions concerning two or more defendants and by necessary right of the principal defendant to be convened first and by right of authority to be divided.

And I, the said Guillelma, expressly certified according to fact and fully advised concerning my competence in law and instructed in the benefit of the *senatusconsultum Velleianum*, by the privilege of my dowry, by the right of my pledge and by the *lex Julia de fundo dotali* of not alienating authentically without the wife's consent and both of us in general with all *bastides* and their privileges and royal statutes and whatever other privileges and statutes having been conceded and to be conceded and every other right of use and custom by which we will be able to come against the abovesaid and any of the above or also direct attention certainly toward, preserve, complete and in nothing contradict or come in law or in fact against each and every thing above through us or through one or another in any way. We promise to you the said buyer as stipulating above and we swear on the holy evangelists touched by us and each of us physically.

Under this aforesaid judgment and by its virtue, we promise and assert that we said, did and admitted nothing, that we will say or do nothing in the future to keep every and each of the aforewritten things from remaining stable and strong.

Enacted in the royal part of Montpellier. These men are the witnesses: Guillelmus Viridarii, cultivator, Andreas Dalmassii, gardener, Johannes Roverani, blacksmith, Guillelmus Holanie, junior clerk of said place, and I, Johannes Holanie, notary written below.

After this year and the day which is written above, I, said Rigaudus de Broa, having certified to the completion of the aforesaid sale and to every and each thing written above, praise,

---

[28]The letter of Emperor Hadrian in question may be that referring to obligations in contracts, notably those of guarantors (*fideiussores*) to pay only their share of a debt.

counsel, and confirm to you, said Bernardus Egidii, present, and for you and your men, stipulating and receiving, this sale and every and each thing written above, acknowledging and recognizing that I have had and received 4 *l.p.t.* from you, counting, the good money having been counted out in the name of this approval. In which I renounce a claim that the money had not been counted out and not received or said consent had not been given.

Enacted in Montpellier. These, aside from the last paragraph, are the witnesses: the aforenamed Guillelmus Viridarii, Andreas Dalmassii, Johannes Roverani, and I, said Johannes Holanie, royal public notary of Montpellier who was ordered and requested, drew up all and every aforesaid thing in this document and signed my sign.

The instrument was extracted.

33. **Sale of a Vineyard (*Venditio*)**: Folios 11v–12r, dated 27 July 1327:

In the year and on the day aforesaid, we, Pontius de Gabiano, draper of Montpellier, and son and universal heir of the late Raymundus de Gabiano, pepperer of Montpellier, and Rixendis, spouses, and Maria and Margarita de Gabiano, sisters of the said Pontius de Gabiano and daughters of the said late Raymundus de Gabiano and the said Rixendis, spouses, we all, the said Pontius, Maria, and Margarita de Gabiano, brother and sisters, asserting through our own oath, given freely and physically upon the holy gospels, that I, the said Pontius, being of legal age at twenty-four years, and that I, the said Maria, being of legal age at eighteen years, and that I, the said Margarita, being of legal age at fourteen years, and that we and each of us separately are without a *curator*, by the wish as well by the counsel and authority and express consent of the said Rixendis, our mother, that I the said Rixendis, mother of the said brother and sisters, confirm to be true.[29] And moreover, I

---

[29]Twenty-five was the age of legal majority in Roman law, but fourteen was the medieval age of practical majority for boys and twelve that for girls.

state and assert through my own oath pledged freely and physically upon the said holy gospels that the said Pontius is of legal age at twenty-four years and the said Maria is of legal age at eighteen years and the said Margarita is of legal age at fourteen years and that these and each of the them are without a *curator*. And in addition, I, the said Maria, at the wish, counsel, license, and authority of Andreas Dionisii, my fiancé, present, which I, the said Andreas Dionisii, fiancé of the said Maria, confirm to be true, and also I, the said Rixendis, the aforesaid mother. We, indeed, all four abovenamed Rixendus, Pontius, Maria, and Margarita de Gabiano, having been made principal sellers of the property mentioned below, together and individually without any party or person being excused, for us and ours, etc. we sell etc. to you, Andreas Corregerii, grain merchant of Montpellier, present and purchasing etc. Moreover, always with the counsel, direct domain, and approval and with the right of first refusal of Lord Pontius Aybrandi, *domicellus* and lord of Saussan, and his successors and with the annual *census* or *usaticum* of 6 *d.t.* to be paid to him and his successors at the feast of Saint Peter in August, namely: our whole vineyard with all ingress, egress and its other appurtenances and rights, located in the *decimaria* of Montels[30] in the place or territory called Podium Bartolaye which adjoins the property of the children of the late Guillelmus Bonerii, and the property of Lord Raymundus de Capite Vilario, *jurisperitus*, and the property of Petrus de Negra Sauhas and the property of Sir Balbianus, which was that of Guillelmus Marcialis. Through the property of said Balbianus, the frontal confront of the vineyard and by access of the same, you have the right to free ingress, egress, and easement of entering and leaving up to the public roadway, with men and animals, loaded and unloaded, and in whatever manner, by day and night, and at any hour. Moreover, for this sale etc., we acknowledge etc. that we have had from you etc., in the name of a just and legal price, 90 good *l.p.t.* Which price etc., concerning which etc. and in the

---

[30]This is the modern Saint-Michel-de-Montels.

aforesaid, we renounce etc. Truly etc. concerning which etc. of which etc. Wishing etc. and until etc. applying etc. ceding etc. And we promise [to you], together and each of us individually, and we agree with you, the said purchaser, as above stipulating and receiving, and through you to yours, that we and each of us and our successors cause you and your successors, and those whom you wish, to have, to hold, and to possess perpetually, peacefully, and quietly all the access rights of the vineyard with the said ingress and egress through the said property of the said Balbianus with all of its appurtenances and rights. And we shall always defend all the access rights to the vineyard with its said ingress, egress, and all of its appurtenances and rights for you and your successors, with us holding forth and protecting [them] in court and out of court at our own expenses and costs, against and in opposition to each and every person in regard to the access rights of the same vineyard, and against any petitions, claims, lawsuits, controversies, or demands made on it or in regard to it in any way. We also promise etc. that each and every person etc. will approve etc. Otherwise etc. About which etc. For which etc. Through each and every eviction etc. We obligate etc. ourselves personally, together and each of us individually, and all our present and future goods, and [those] of each of us individually. Under the strength of the jurisdiction and coercion of the seal of Montpellier in the court of the said lord king of the French and of Navarre etc. We promise and swear etc.

Enacted in Montpellier. These are the witnesses: Berengarius de Valle Buxeria, Guiraudus Rays, furriers, Georgius Stephani, cultivator, Johannes Vilas, baker of the said place, and I, etc.

After this, on the day and in the year above, almost immediately after the sale, I, Raymundus de Gabiano, son of the said late Raymundus de Gabiano, having certified etc. to you, the said Andreas Corregerii, present, etc. approve etc. and whatever of right and action etc. I promise and swear etc. Enacted in Montpellier. These are the witnesses from the paragraph above: the said Georgius Stephani, Johannes Vilas, and I etc.

After this, on the day and in the year aforesaid, I, Petrus de Gabiano, son of said late Raymundus de Gabiano, having certified etc. to you, the said Andreas Corregerii, present, etc. approve etc. and whatever of right and action etc. I promise and swear etc. Enacted in Montpellier. These, from the nearby paragraph above, are the witnesses: the said Georgius Stephani, Johannes Vilas, and I etc.

After this, in the above year and on the thirtieth day of the month of July, with the same Lord Charles [reigning] etc., I, Symon de Tornaforti, public notary of Montpellier and also the *procurator* and, in the name of *procurator* for that written below, of the Lord Pontius Aybrandi, with the instrument made thereupon by Johannes Calbayroni, public notary of Montpellier, having certified etc. to you, the said Andreas Corregerii, present etc., approve in the name of the above procuration etc. Confirming etc. that I have had from you etc. in the name of this approval 9 *l.t.* etc. Witnesses: Petrus Fabre, Guiraudus Calverti, inhabitants of Montpellier, and I etc.

The instrument was extracted.

Approvals of Land Sales

A *laudatio* (approval) contract was a medieval contract in which the ultimate owner of property approves and consents to the sale or other alienation of property. The *laudatio* contract is indicative of a very complex structure of ownership rights, where a seller of a parcel of real estate might not have been, and probably was not, the sole or ultimate owner of the property, but where the sale was actually the transfer of a lease or possessory rights. A *laudatio* contract was also given as a consent to an alienation by heirs who might have a future ownership interest in property. The *laudatio* contract (Document 34) relates to the sale of land and houses in Document 32 above. The claim of family members to landed property was very strong, and their consent was necessary in the disposal of that property. This type of consent contract theoretically precludes a family member from later suing or claiming his/her property rights. *Laudatio* contracts are a rich source of information on types of property ownership, on family and social relationships, and on religious donations. Note again, as in the above document, that the property is described by its relationship to other neighboring property.

34. Approval of a Land Sale (*Laudatio*): Folio 3r–v, dated 9 July 1327:

In the year and on the day above, I, Jacoba, wife of Bertrandus Firmeti, tailor of Montpellier, present, willing and authorized that I, said Bertrandus Firmeti, husband of this Jacoba, acknowledge this to be true: I, said Jacoba, having completely certified that a certain sale was made to you Bernardus Egidii, gardener of Montpellier by Stephanus Sospontis, my brother, and by Guillelma, his wife: namely of one garden with four houses contiguous with the garden and with a third part of a well which is next to said garden in another garden of my cousin Stephanus Sospontis, situated in the town suburbs of Montpellier behind the house and church of the Templars, now of the Order of Saint John of Jerusalem, and bordering on one side with the kitchen garden of said house formerly of the Templars, with the public road in the middle, and on the other side with the garden of the other Stephanus Sospontis and with the garden of Bertrandus Caponi, gardener, and with the garden of Johannes Menatoris, pepperer, with the town wall in the middle. Accordingly, said sale of late stands firm through an instrument prepared by the notary signed below in the year above and on the seventh day of the month of July.

Therefore, I consent, approve, commend, ratify, and confirm said sale, and every and each thing contained in it, to you said Bernardus Egidii, being present, and for you and your men, stipulating and receiving. And whatever rights and authority in the aforesaid garden, four houses, and a third part of a well I have or I ought to have, for whatever reason or cause, I cede and entrust to you and your men. And I promise and swear upon the Holy Gospels, physically and freely touched by me, that I will never act against every and each aforesaid thing or cause someone else to do so in whatever way, stipulating to you as above. Renouncing, therefore, all rights, uses and customs

(*consuetudines*) whatsoever against the aforesaid or whatever
rights I may come to possess or may hold.

Enacted in Montpellier. These men are the witnesses:
Johannes Ronerani, Jacobus de Avinione, furrier of said place,
and I, Johannes Holanie, a royal public notary of Montpellier
who was ordered and requested to write this.

Rentals

The term *locatio* could refer to the operations of hiring or leasing
of both goods, movable and immovable, and of services. In the case of
land or houses, *locatio* is used in the Montpellier documents to indicate
short-term rental of months or years, but for a fixed term, rather than
long-term leasing which was termed *emphyteusis*. Rents were usually in
money. The lessee did not have possessory rights in the property, but
the lessor was liable if the lessee were evicted.

35. **Rental of a House (*Locatio*)**: Folio 135r–v, dated
    9 March 1328 (n.s.):
    In the aforesaid year and on the ninth day of the month
    of March, Lord Philip etc. reigning, I, Jacobus Egidii, gold-
    smith of Montpellier etc., rent etc. to you, Aymericus de Sancto
    Egidio, money-changer of said place, present etc., namely: one
    whole house (*hospitium*) of mine located inside the town of
    Montpellier in the *insula* of the hospital of the Lord Bishop
    of Agde, adjoining the house of the children of the late Johannes
    de Cruce and the house of Petrus Romei for his wife, and the
    public road. Moreover, I make this rental etc. from the next
    feast of Blessed Virgin in mid-August for the next two con-
    tinuous and complete years and for the term of payment or
    rent each year of the said two years 12 *l.t.* which you will give
    and pay to me according to the customary terms and pay-
    ments in the town of Montpellier, namely: half at the first day
    of Shrovetide [Lent] and the other half at the feast of the
    Blessed Virgin in mid-August. And thus I promise etc. Other-
    wise I promise to return etc. all damages etc. For which etc. I
    obligate etc. myself and all my present and future goods, and

I promise especially and expressly the border rights of the aforesaid house etc.

And consequently etc., I, said Aymericus de Sancto Egidio . . . .

Enacted in Montpellier. Witnesses: Petrus Cayssani, goldsmith, Bernardus Ricardi, merchant of said place, and I etc.

After this, in the year of the Lord 1329 and on the twelfth day of October, said Jacobus Egidii acknowledged to said Aymericus de Sancto Egidio, present etc., that said Aymericus had satisfied him in the aforesaid 12 *l.t.* for both of the said two years etc. and for each year etc. and for the whole said rent which obligated said Aymericus and all his goods. Through faith etc. Witnesses: Thomas Cayssarii, goldsmith, G. Telherie.

After this, in the year of our Lord 1329 and on the 17th day of March, this whole note was cancelled at the wish of the parties. Witnesses: Thomas Caysani, Bernardus Aurioli.

Long-Term Leases

An *emphyteusis* (*emphitheosis*) is a long-term lease of land for which the leaseholder paid fixed rents and/or taxes. The leaseholder in this type of land lease had similar rights to those of a landowner and enjoyed all the benefits accrued from the use of the land. Land held under this type of lease could be held in perpetuity, or it could be alienated or transferred by sale or testament. The term *accapitum* had a variety of meanings when used in association with land: it could refer to a purchase, a land tenure, or lease of land. By the thirteenth century, the term *accapitum* was often used interchangeably with the term *emphyteusis* to mean a long-term holding or lease of land.

36. Recognition of Land Tenure by Long-Term Lease (*Emphyteusis*): Folio 72r, dated 6 November 1327:

In the year and on the day aforesaid, I, Johanna, daughter of the late Petrus Ruffi, gardener of Montpellier, wife of Dyonsius Deodati, cultivator of the said place, etc. acknowledge etc. to you Guillelmus de Lineris, cultivator of the said place, my brother-in-law, present, etc. that I have and hold from you in *emphyteusis* and under you and your successors by direct domain, counsel, approval and the right of first refusal and revenue or yearly tax of 2 *d.m.* to be paid to you and your successors every year at the Paschal feast of the Lord [Easter]; namely: my one entire piece of garden with all rights of ingress, egress, and other appurtenances and its rights coming to me from this division made among me and Jacoba and Maria, my sisters, concerning this garden situated in the suburbs of the royal quarter of Montpellier; the aforesaid piece of the garden adjoins a piece of garden of my sister Jacoba coming from the garden in the aforesaid division and a piece of garden of the said Maria, my sister, from the said division, and the garden of the Friars Minor of Montpellier, with a pathway in the middle, and with the garden of Johannes Grossi, the Aygarella [the *Aiguerelle noire* stream] in the middle.[31] And I promise etc. For which etc. I obligate etc. myself and all my present and future goods etc. especially and expressly my aforefronted garden. Thus etc.

Enacted in Montpellier. Witnesses: the aforesaid above. The instrument was extracted.

37. Grant of House Tenure by Long-Term Lease (*Accapitum*): Folio 72v, dated 7 November 1327:

In the year and on the day aforesaid, I, Alazacia de Cruzolis, wife of the late Jacobus de Cruzolis, merchant of Montpellier, and also as mother and legal administrator of my children and of my said late husband, having fully sought the truth through me in the name of my said [children] with you, Johannes Oliverii, alias Pauli, wood merchant of Montpellier etc., having sought etc., having performed in addition a personal oath physically etc. Therefore etc., I give etc. in the name of said children etc., on account of the absence of instruments

---

[31]The *Aiguerelle noire* was one of two streams that crossed Montpellier in the Middle Ages.

in *accapitum*, anew etc. to you, said Johannes Pauli, alias Oliverii, present etc., always, moreover, with my rights and [those of] my children and their successors of counsel, direct domain, approval, and first refusal and the revenue or tax of 8 *d.t.* to be paid to my same children and their successors every year at the feast of Saint Michael, namely: one entire house with all foundations, walls, roof, water falling from the eaves of the house, with ingress, egress and other appurtenances, and its rights, situated in the suburbs of the royal quarter of Montpellier in the place called Las Barcas which adjoins the house of Johannes Garnerii, draper, and with the house of Lord Petrus Tibiaudi, priest, and with the house of Lady Beatrissa and with the public road. This etc., saving the right of my said children and also of another, acknowledging etc. that I had from you in the name of my said children [and] in the name of this new *accapitum* two hens. In which I renounce etc. and under my obligation and of all the goods of mine and of my said children, present and future with everything. Renouncing etc. and swearing through faith etc.

Enacted in Montpellier. These are the witnesses: Raymundus Caslarii, butcher, Guiraudus Bugaderii, broker of Montpellier, and I etc.

The instrument was extracted.

Barter

A barter contract (*scambium*) is another type of exchange contract, which involved the exchange of one thing for another thing but generally did not involve the exchange of money. However, note that the barter contract below does include the payment of a monetary amount in order to make up the difference in values between the properties exchanged. Barter contracts delineated the names of the parties involved and the terms of the exchange of property. The following contract involved the exchange of real property, but it could have just as easily involved the exchange of animals or personal property.

38. Land Exchange or Barter (*Scambium*): Folio 85r–v, dated
3 December 1327:

In the year and on the day aforesaid, I, Maria, daughter
of the late Petrus de Sobremon, tanner of Montpellier, and wife
of Stephanus Genesii, cultivator of the said place, etc. promise
or exchange etc. with you, Firminus Valerie, mercer of Montpellier, present etc. Moreover, with the counsel, direct domain,
approval, and right of first approval of Petrus Columberii,
merchant of Montpellier, and of his successors, and for a revenue
or tax of 6 *d.t.* to be paid to the same man and his successors
every year at the feast of Saint Peter in August; namely my
one entire piece of field, with all the entrances and exits and
other appurtenances and rights thereto, purchased by me with
money had from certain of my *parafernalia* which came to me
from my late mother, Lady Johanna; which aforesaid piece of
field is located in the place or territory called Dabian and bor-
ders the possession of Bertrandus and Petrus Genesii, brothers,
and the possession of Hugo de Caranta, with the public road
in the middle, and the possession of Bernardus Columberii
and the possession of Johannes Bonafossii, cultivator. And I
acknowledge and recognize to you as stipulating above, that for
the exchange and in the name of the exchange of the aforefronted piece of field that you gave and changed and exchanged today and immediately with me your one entire piece
of a vineyard located in the place or territory called Noals,
fronting with the possession of Bertrandus Gauterii and with
the possession of Raymundus Bona Cara and with the route of
Montaubérou and with the possession of Guillelmus Michaelis,
with the public road between them. In order that said exchange made by you of the aforefronted piece of vineyard be
legitimate, it is done through an instrument made or received
by the notary noted below in the year and on the day above.
And also I acknowledge and recognize to you, as stipulating
above, that, in order to settle accounts and for the greater value
of the piece of aforefronted field exchanged by me to you, you
gave and paid to me in good counted money 34 *l.p.t.* And

concerning which piece of vineyard and the aforesaid 34 *l.p.t.*, I consider myself satisfied and content in exchange for the property from you. And concerning the aforesaid, I renounce etc. truly etc. concerning the same aforefronted piece of vineyard etc. And of which etc. wishing etc. and until etc. and further doing etc. ceding etc. And I promise etc. that etc. all of the aforefronted piece of field etc. I will make you have [it] forever, etc. And I promise also etc. that each and every person etc. will consent etc. Another etc. Concerning which etc. For which etc. And from every eviction etc. I obligate etc. myself and all my present and future goods etc. especially and expressly the aforefronted piece of my vineyard exchanged through you to me. Refusing special obligations etc. I renounce etc., promise, and swear etc.

And without delay, I, said Petrus Columberii, merchant of Montpellier, etc. approve for you, said Firminius Valerie present etc., acknowledging that I have had from you, in the name of this approval, 6 *l.p.t.* Concerning which I renounce etc. And moreover, having inquired most completely into the truth with you, the said Firminius Valerie, etc.; having inquired also etc., with that conceded above by you with a physical oath etc. Therefore, I give etc. in new *accapitum* etc., on account of the missing instruments, to you said Firminus Valerie present etc. with direct domain, counsel, approval, the right of first refusal, and the aforesaid revenue or tax to me and my successors, namely: the whole piece of aforefronted field with all of the entrances, exits, and other appurtenances and its rights whatsoever. This etc. Acknowledging etc. that I have had from you etc. in the name of this new *accapitum* two pairs of hens. In which I renounce etc. through faith etc.

Enacted in Montpellier. All these aforesaid men are witnesses: Lord Andreas de Autinhaco, priest, Laurentius de Cruce, draper, Guillelmus Michaelis, mercer, Johannes Rossini, cultivator of the said place, and I, Johannes Holanie, etc.

After this, in the year and on the day above. I, said Stephanus Genesii, spouse of the said Maria, confirming in truth and publicly recognizing that the above aforefronted piece of field had been formerly bought by the said Maria, my wife, from money [she] had from the same dotal goods of hers, coming to her from her late mother, the said Johanna. Having certified etc. to you, the said Firminus Valerie, present etc., I approve etc. and I promise and swear etc. whatever of right and action etc.

Enacted in the suburbs of the town of Montpellier. Those of the above paragraph are witnesses: said Johannes Rossini, Guillelmus Johannis, bleacher of the said place, and I etc.

The instrument was extracted.

Usufruct

The term usufruct or *ususfructus* means the right to use property and the right to all the produce from the property. It is important to remember that the right of usufruct did not constitute ownership of the land itself, since the owner of the land would still be able to alienate the land without affecting the right of usufruct.

39. **Sale of Usufruct (*Ususfructus*)**: Folio 71r–v, dated 6 November 1327:

In the year and on the day aforesaid, we, Petrus de Corberie, merchant of Montpellier, and Petrus de Corberie of Lattes,[32] and Marcilia, wife of the said Petrus de Corberie of Lattes, all three together and each of us individually through wish and consent etc., sell etc. to you, Bernardus Marti of Lattes, present etc., namely: all and each revenue, *ususfructus*, proceeds, goods, enjoyment, and profit of one whole garden of ours and of all its trees and of one house erected on it, namely: with all its appurtenances and rights, situated below the walls of the *castrum* of Lattes, which adjoins the surrounding wall of the said fortified town of Lattes and the public road which runs toward the mill of the said *castrum* and the

---

[32]Lattes is an ancient port and a small town, located between Montpellier and the inland waterways leading to the Mediterranean.

wall of the mill, with the road in the middle. Moreover, we make this sale etc. to you, receiving, for the next four continuous and complete years from today and for the universal price of the whole said time 15 *l.p.t.* which we had from you etc. In which we renounce etc. truly etc. We will make etc. to have etc. Otherwise etc. For which etc. we obligate etc. ourselves together and each of us individually and all our present and future goods. We renounce etc. We promise and swear etc. Under which aforesaid oath and obligation we promise you, stipulating above and agree that the said house, erected in the said garden, and the walls of said house, namely: we will hold for you and yours the condominium and the accommodation for the whole garden for the entire said time at our own costs and expenses.

Enacted in Montpellier. These are the witnesses: Johannes Pauli, alias Oliverii, wood merchant of Montpellier, Raymundus Duranti, blacksmith, Pontius de Salsano of Lattes, and I etc.

Sharecropping

Grants of land in *meiaria* or sharecropping, lasting from four to six years, were less permanent than those in *accapitum* or in *emphyteusis*. Sharecropping was a form of agricultural credit, with land provided by the lessor to the lessee, in return for half the harvest. Risks involved were generally shared, and contracts might specify particular tasks which the lessee was to perform in regard to the planting, cultivating, and harvesting of certain crops.

40. Sharecropping Contract (*Meiaria*): Folio 53v, dated 5 October 1327:

In the aforesaid year and on the fifth day of the month of October, Lord Charles [reigning] etc., I, Guillelmus Tota Buons, money-changer of Montpellier etc., give etc. in *meiariam* etc. to you, Stephanus de Bagiis, miller of Montpellier, present, etc., namely: my one whole piece of field situated in the place called Costa Bela which adjoins two possessions of

Deodatus Arrebati, with the wall in the middle, and one other possession of mine, and the public road. Moreover, I make etc. this sharecropping agreement etc. from now until the next future feast of Saint Peter in August and under the agreements, law, and conventions which follow: first, that you will cause the said piece of field to be planted in those grains which seem appropriate to you and cause the fruits of the grain to be reaped and to have the said grain made into hay and to have these same grains transported to the thrashing ground at your expenses and there in the thrashing ground you will give to me or mine a whole half in entirety of the aforesaid grain with the exception of the oats which you ought to plant in the upper part of the said field which oats may be yours and all of the chaff may be yours. And thus I promise etc. Otherwise etc. For which etc. I obligate etc. myself and all my present and future goods. I renounce etc., promise through faith etc.

And consequently, I, the said Stephanus . . . .

Witnesses: Dionisius Albini, cultivator, Guillelmus Holanie the younger, cleric of said place, and I etc.

GLOSSARY

(Foreign-language terms are italicized)

accapitum—a long-term lease in Montpellier contracts; at times a hereditary lease elsewhere in the south of France.

acquittal—an acknowledgement of repayment of debt or satisfaction of obligation.

actum, acta—an act, acts; the notarial instrument was often called an *actum*.

agneaux (*agnels*)—French royal gold coins.

allod—freehold tenure.

amicabilis compositio—amicable settlement of a dispute.

ancilla—domestic servant, sometimes unfree.

area—a threshing floor.

atelier—a workshop; in the present context, a notarial workshop.

augmentum—gift from groom to bride to augment the dowry.

bastide—fortified town founded in southwestern France along the border separating French and English holdings prior to the Hundred Years' War.

breve—a short form or brief note (*nota breve*) of a notarial act, often written on a loose scrap of paper, which accounts for limited survival; contains only the minimum contract information.

calculus Florentinus style—a dating style for documents, common in medieval southern Europe, in which the calendar year began on 25 March; the result of a New Year on 25 March is that dates from 1 January–14 March have been converted to the following year, with the notation "n. s.," meaning "new style."

carteriata—measure of land based on its productive capacity.

cartulary or chartulary—a term used in many contexts, implying a collection of documents. For the notarial context, a notarial register, see **register**.

castrum—fortified town.

causa cambii—by reason of money exchange; a phrase used to indicate why obligation existed.

causa mutui—by reason of a loan; a phrase used to indicate why indebtedness existed.

census—dues from land owed to the holder of eminent domain.

commenda—a partnership with differing terms, often with an investing partner who contributed capital and a traveling partner who contributed labor, with the division of profits 3/4 for the investing partner and 1/4 for the traveling partner; called in the local Montpellier documents *comanda*.

confiteor me debere vobis—recognition of debt; literally: "I acknowledge that I owe to you."

consuetudines—customs.

consul—a representative of the executive branch of municipal government in the consular regimes of the south of France and Italy; in Montpellier, one of twelve such representatives.

consulate—a form of municipal government, common to southern France and Italy in the Middle Ages.

contract—a legally binding engagement with obligations of a monetary, personal, or legal sort.

corpus—the body (central section) of a notarial act.

curator—similar to a guardian (*tutor*) but usually in regard to a ward over fourteen.

datum—date; the dating clause of a notarial act, part of the *protocol*.

decimaria—tithing district.

deed—a legally valid contract of ownership of real estate.

d. (*denarius*)—a penny or *denier*, a common denomination of medieval coinage and for a long time the only coin which was actually minted.

d.m. (*denarius melgoriensium*)—the local coinage of the region of Montpellier, named for Melgueil (Mauguio), the site of the original mint; enjoyed a wide circulation in the south of France and was relatively stable in value over time.

d.t. (*denarius turonensium*)—Tournois penny; see *l.p.t.* and *l.t.*

denesium—land with restricted use.

domicellus, domicelli—young nobleman (men).

dominium directum—direct domain or eminent domain, meaning abstract property rights.

donatio inter vivos—a bequest during the lifetime of the donor (giver) to the beneficiary (recipient).

dos—dowry; money and/or property that a woman brings to a marriage; a dowry contract.

draper—cloth merchant, a prestigious medieval profession.

emphyteusis (*emphitheosis*)—a long-term or hereditary lease of real estate property; see *accapitum*.

emptio—a contract of purchase by either cash or credit.

episcopal—referring to a bishop.

eschatocol—ending or conclusion of a contract, with witnesses and the notarial signature, followed perhaps by a note that the contract had been extracted or cancelled.

exceptio non numeratae (et non traditae) pecuniae[1]—a renunciation of Roman law acknowledging that money owed had not been paid; normally an action protecting the debtor.

Extractum est instrumentum—"The instrument has been extracted."

eymina (*emina*)—a measure of capacity.

eyminata—measure of land, based on its productive capacity.

factor—a business agent, used frequently by the large Italian merchant banking companies such as the Bardi and the Peruzzi of Florence.

garhilfilatum—spiced wine; a wine seasoned with cloves.

giroflé (*garofolum*)—cloves.

grossus—the extended form of a notarial act, written out for clients who made the request for a personal copy.

hospitium—house.

hypotheca—pledge; a type of real security.

Incarnation dating style—this chronology began the year on 25 March, literally from the incarnation of Christ, *ab incarnatione*; the result, as in the *calculus Florentinus* style was for the period 1 January to 24 March to be included in the previous year. Hence, in conversion to modern dating, the designation "n. s." ("new style") is appended to dates in that period.

incipit—beginning words of a manuscript text.

instrumentum, instrumenta—notarial act(s).

insula—a sector of urban space.

jurisperitus—jurist, one learned in the law.

laudatio—a formal approval of the sale of real estate by someone with legal interest.

---

[1]The dipthong drops out in medieval Latin.

lex Julia de fundo dotali—Roman law prohibition of a husband's alienation of dotal land without his wife's consent.

l. (*libra, librarum*)—pound(s); a monetary unit of coinage.

librarum melgoriensium—Melgorian coins, minted at Melgueil (present-day Mauguio); stable coinage of Languedoc.

l.p.t. (*librarum turonensium parvorum* or *livres petits tournois*)—Tournois coins; French royal coinage of Tours.

l.t. (*librarum turonensium* or *livres tournois*)—Tournois coins; money of account.

locatio—a rental.

mansus—*mas*, a center of agricultural exploitation.

mark—a unit of weight or value of gold or silver.

meiaria—a sharecropping agreement.

miles, milites—knight(s).

minute book—collection of notarial minutes in a register.

money of account—system of standardized computation or accounting whereby 12 pennies equal one shilling; 20 shillings equal one pound; thus 240 pennies equal one pound, regardless of actual precious metal content.

mutuum—a loan.

nota—a short notarial act; see *breve.*

notarius—a notary.

palherium—chaff loft.

parafernalia—goods, often personal items such as clothing, in addition to the dowry, which a woman brought into a marriage. She retained control over these dotal goods.

p.t. (*petits tournois*)—Tournois coinage, actually coined.

preceptor—teacher, administrator.

pro cambio—by reason of exchange; a phrase common in money exchange contracts.

procuratio—procuration; a delegation of authority through legal representation, with specific or general mandate to act.

procurator, procuratores—legal representative(s).

pro forma—as a matter of form.

protocol—the introductory section of a notarial act with information such as the date and the political authority under which the contract was written; *protocolla* refer to notarial chartularies or registers; the term for notarial registers in Spanish archives is *protocolos*.

réaux (regales)—royals; gold coins.

register—the assemblage, sometimes called a cartulary (chartulary), of notarial acts written by one or more notaries, including a minute book like Holanie's.

Romania—Byzantine Empire.

saumata—a measure of capacity.

sceaux rigoureux—French royal courts of voluntary jurisdiction, particularly applicable to the new economy of trade and finance in medieval towns; examples include the court of the wardens of the Champagne fairs, the court of the *Petit Scel* in Montpellier, and the *Cour des Conventions* in Nîmes.

scambium—an exchange or barter.

senatusconsultum Velleianum—a Roman law which protected women from being forced to assume obligations for other persons, notably the debts of their husbands; its renunciation in notarial contracts freed women from this constraint and permitted them to assume liabilities for others.

sestariata—measure of land based on its productive capacity.

sétier (sestarius or sextarius)—a measure of capacity; the *sétier* of Montpellier was the equivalent of 48.92 liters.

s.t. (*sous tournois*)—Tournois shilling, money of account.

tabellio—under Rome, a private person who wrote documents for private people; one of the precedents for the medieval notary.

tabularius—under Rome, a fiscal official concerned primarily with taxes; one of the precedents for the medieval notary.

usance—repayment term in a money exchange.

usaticum—a land revenue.

usufruct/*ususfructus*—the right of use; the income (fruits) derived from such use; often referring to the revenues produced from real estate.

usury—in the Middle Ages any interest on a loan or other credit transaction; today refers to exorbitant interest.

venditio (*vendicio*)—a contract of sale, either cash or credit.

vicarius—the political authority of a subdivision (*vicaria*) of a county.

NOTE ON MODERN NOTARIES

The functions of the modern notary public in the United States in commerce and real estate resemble those of the medieval notary, though important dimensions of the traditional recording role of the notary have been assumed by attorneys in the United States.[1] To attest to the authenticity of the signatures on a written document, the U.S. notary's job is to verify the identity of the parties before they sign a contract and to witness their signatures. The notary also administers oaths and then attests to the same (a *jurat*). The notary may ask signers to swear that they are signing of free will (California, Louisiana, and Florida).[2]

The notarial signature and seal then constitute legal proof that the parties really did appear before the notary and sign the document. The notary's signature and seal form part of a legal affidavit attached to the document. The modern notary serves as the "witness" to the signatures and can be called to testify in court. All documents affecting property ownership, such as deeds, liens, and mortgages, need to be notarized. No piece of real estate can be transferred in the United States without a valid notarial affidavit. Certain documents, such as affidavits, subpoenas, depositions, powers of attorney, and wills, and absentee ballots for voting abroad, require notarization.

---

[1] For more information, see the National Notary Association.

[2] The differing historical experience of states in the U. S. affects their notarial tradition. Spanish influence has affected states such as Florida, Louisiana, and California while French presence has had a significant impact on law in Louisiana, in particular.

Notaries public in the United States are authorized to perform their duties by each individual state. In the state of Minnesota notaries must be free of felony convictions and be bonded. Technically, they are considered officers of the court or of the state. Some states require that a notarial journal be kept (e.g., Oregon and Florida). There are written exams for notaries in some states. In some jurisdictions it is necessary to be a practicing attorney before becoming a notary. States regulate the fees notaries can charge for their services. For the most part, these duties are similar in every state, but two states, namely Florida and Virginia, have authorized notaries public to perform additional duties. In Florida, a notary public can perform marriages ceremonies; in Virginia, a notary public is also a peace officer. Some states allow notaries to draft notarial testaments and acts of donation, and to make inventories, appraisals, and marriage contracts, as well as to be named as administrator, executor, and trustee. Yet, in the United States, the role of the notary public is relatively minor compared to the functions exercised by the medieval notary and by the modern continental European notary, as the notarial tradition preserves a strong legal role, undiminished its contractual function, in countries such as France and Italy.

In present-day Europe notaries enjoy favorable social and economic status as members of the legal profession, as do judges, magistrates, and lawyers, much as they did in the Middle Ages. A university law degree and apprenticeship as a clerk in the office of notaries are necessary before one can become a notary in France, Italy, and Spain. The notarial office passes down in families as a valuable asset of the family fortune, and there is often succession from father to son over many generations in a particular notarial firm. Today, the purchase of a notarial firm with an already established clientele is a costly undertaking.

SUGGESTIONS FOR FURTHER READING

Much of the scholarship using notarial sources is European and is found in languages other than English. This is true of source publication and of secondary studies. Moreover, most of the surviving notarial registers of southern Europe remain unpublished in archives such as those of Montpellier (Archives départementales de l'Hérault, II E 95, and Archives municipales de Montpellier, BB), Perpignan (Archives départementales de Pyrénées-Orientales, Series E), and Valencia (Archivo del Reino de Valencia, protocolos). There have been some editions of acts and some detailed inventories and synopses of acts, notably for Genoese notaries, such as Giovanni Scriba. See Mario Chiaudano and Mattia Moresco, eds., *Il Cartolare di Giovanni Scriba*, 2 vols. (Turin: S. Lattes and Co., 1935; rpt. Bottega d'Erasmo, 1970). In the 1930s and early 1940s, Robert L. Reynolds of the University of Wisconsin directed an American initiative to publish early Genoese registers. Examples include M. W. Hall, H. G. Krueger, and R. L. Reynolds, eds., *Guglielmo Cassinese (1190–1192)*, 2 vols. (Genoa/Turin, 1938); M. W. Hall-Cole, H. G. Krueger, R. G. Reinest, and R. L. Reynolds, eds., *Giovanni di Guiberto (1200–1211)*, 2 vols. (Turin, 1939–40); and J. E. Eierman, H. G. Krueger, and R. L. Reynolds, eds., *Bonvillano (1198)* (Turin, 1939). Later Genoese acts can be found in Renée Doehaerd, *Les relations commerciales entre Gênes, la Belgique et l'Outremont d'après les archives notariales génoises aux XIIIe et XIVe siècles*, vols. I–III (Brussels, Rome: Institut historique belge de Rome, 1941); and L. L. de Sturler, *Les relations commerciales entre Gênes, la Belgique et l'Outremont d'après les archives notariales génoises, 1200–1400*, 2 vols. (Brussels, 1962). More recently, there have been editions of Genoese notaries practicing in the eastern Mediterranean world. An example is V. Polonio, ed., *Notai genovesi in Oltremare. Atti rogati a Cipro da Lamberto di Sambuceto (3 Luglio–3 Augusto 1301)* (Genoa, 1982). Other Italian archival holdings are described by Robert S. Lopez, "The Unexplored Wealth of the Notarial Archives in Pisa and Lucca," *Mélanges offerts à Louis Halphen* (Paris: Presses Universitaires de France, 1951), 417–32. Lopez and Irving W. Raymond published an invaluable source collection, including many notarial acts, as *Medieval Trade in the Mediterranean World. Illustrative Documents Translated with Introductions and Notes* (New York and London: Columbia University Press, 1955, 1961).

A very useful guide to Provençal notaries is John Pryor, *Business Contracts of Medieval Provence. Selected Notulae from the Cartulary of Giraud Amalric of Marseille (1248)* (Toronto: Pontifical Institute of Mediaeval Studies, 1981). Early notarial survivals at Marseille were published by Louis Blancard, ed., *Documents inédits sur le commerce de Marseille au moyen-âge*, 2 vols. (Marseille: Typ. Barlatier-Feissat père et fils, 1884–85). Roger Aubenas, *Documents notariés provençaux du XIIIe siècle* (Aix-en-Provence: Editions du Feu, 1935), also provided published Provençal sources. On Jewish notaries, see Robert I. Burns, *The Jews in the Notarial Culture: Latinate Wills in Mediterranean Spain, 1250–1350* (Berkeley-Los Angeles: University of California Press, 1996), and Joseph Shatzmiller, *Recherches sur la communauté juive de Manosque au Moyen Age, 1240–1329* (Paris: Mouton, 1973).

For a synoptic inventory of notarial registers in the Municipal Archives of Montpellier see *Archives de la ville de Montpellier*, vol. XIII: *Inventaire analytique. Série BB (Notaires et greffiers du consulat 1293–1387)*, ed. Maurice de Dainville, Marcel Gouron, and Liberto Valls (Montpellier: Imprimerie Coopérative Ouvrière l'Abeille, 1984). For southern French holdings, see André Gouron, "Les archives notariales des anciens pays de droit écrit au moyen âge," *Recueil de mémoires et travaux publié par la société d'histoire du droit et des institutions des anciens pays de droit écrit*, fasc. 5 (Montpellier, 1966), 47–60. See also Jan Rogozinski, "Notarial Archives in Southern France in the Fourteenth Century," *French Historical Studies* 7 (1971): 111–16.

On notaries in northern Europe, see James M. Murray, "Failure of corporation: Notaries public in medieval Bruges," *Journal of Medieval History* 12 (1986): 155–66, and *Notarial Instruments in Flanders between 1280 and 1452* (Brussels: Commission Royale d'Histoire/Koninklijke Commissie voor Geschiedenis, 1995). On the English practice, one can consult James Cowie Brown, *The Origin and Early History of the Office of Notary* (Edinburgh: W. Green & Son, Limited, 1936); C. R. Cheney, *Notaries Public in England in the Thirteenth and Fourteenth Centuries* (Oxford: University Press, 1972). The most useful study of English records is that of M. T. Clanchy, *From Memory to Written Record. England 1066–1307* (Oxford and Cambridge, Mass.: Blackwell Publishers, 1979, 1993). For French notaries see Roger Aubenas, *Etude sur le notariat provençal au moyen-âge et sous l'ancien régime* (Aix-en-Provence: Editions du Feu, 1931).

Pathbreaking studies of social and economic history by scholars who have worked on European notarial sources include Richard W. Emery, *The Jews of Perpignan in the Thirteenth Century. An Economic Study Based on Notarial Records* (New York: Columbia University Press, 1959); David Herlihy, *Pisa in the Early Renaissance* (New Haven: Yale University Press, 1958); Raymond de Roover, *Money, Banking and Credit in Mediaeval Bruges: Italian Merchant-Bankers, Lombards and Money-Changers* (Cambridge, Mass.: Harvard Unversity Press, 1948); Philippe Wolff, *Commerces et marchands de Toulouse (vers 1350–vers 1450)* (Paris: Plon, 1954); and the recent work by Daniel Lord Smail, *Imaginary Cartographies. Possession and Identity in Late Medieval Marseille* (Ithaca and London: Cornell University Press, 1999). For further exploration of notarial culture see Kathryn L. Reyerson and John Drendel, eds., *Urban and Rural Communities in Medieval France. Provence & Languedoc, 1000–1500* (Leiden: E. J. Brill, 1998); Kathryn L. Reyerson, *Business, Banking and Finance in Medieval Montpellier* (Toronto: Pontifical Institute of Mediaeval Studies, 1985); Kathryn L. Reyerson, *The Art of the Deal: Intermediaries of Trade in Medieval Montpellier* (Leiden: E. J. Brill, 2001); and Kathryn L. Reyerson, *Society, Law, and Trade in Medieval Montpellier* (Aldershot, Hampshire: Variorum, 1995). See also the studies of Louis de Charrin, *Les testaments de Montpellier au moyen âge* (Ambilly: Coopérative Les Presses de Savoie, 1961); Andrée Courtemanche, *La richesse des femmes. Patrimoines et gestion à Manosque au*

XIVe siècle (Montreal: Bellarmin; Paris: Vrin, 1993); Michel Hébert, *Tarascon au XIVe siècle. Histoire d'une communauté urbaine provençale* (Aix-en-Provence: Edisud, 1979); Jean Hilaire, *Le régime des biens entre époux dans la région de Montpellier du début du XIIIe siècle à la fin du XVIe siècle* (Montpellier: Imprimerie Causse, Graille et Castelnau, 1957); Paul-Louis Malausséna, *La vie en Provence orientale aux XIVe et XVe siècles. Un example: Grasse à travers les actes notariés* (Paris: Librairie Générale de Droit et de Jurisprudence, 1969); and Francine Michaud, *Un signe des temps: accroissement des crises familiales autour du patrimoine à Marseille à la fin du XIIIe siècle* (Toronto: Pontifical Institute of Mediaeval Studies, 1994).

The diplomatics of medieval sources, including notarial registers, can be explored in Leonard E. Boyle, "Diplomatics," in James M. Powell, ed., *Medieval Studies, an Introduction* (Syracuse: Syracuse University Press, 1976, 1993). See also Roger Aubenas, *Cours d'histoire du droit privé des anciens pays de droit écrit (XIIIe–XIVe siècles)*, vol. I: *Contrats et obligations d'après les actes de la pratique* (Aix-en-Provence: Librairie de l'Université, 1954), and Alain de Boüard, *Manuel de diplomatique française et pontificale*, 2 vols. (Paris: Picard, 1948). See also Alfred Giry, *Manuel de diplomatique* (Paris: Librairie Hachette, 1896). On notarial abbreviations see Auguste Dumas, "Dieu nous garde de l'*et cetera* du notaire," in *Mélanges Paul Fournier* (Paris: Recueil Sirey, 1929), 153–69. On Roman law renunciations in notarial sources see Peter Riesenberg, "Roman Law, Renunciations and Business in the Twelfth and Thirteenth Centuries," in *Essays in Medieval Life and Thought Presented in Honor of Austin Patterson Evans*, ed. John Hine Mundy et al. (New York: Columbia University Press, 1955), 207–25. Edmondo Meynial, "De l'application du droit romain dans la région de Montpellier aux XIIe et XIIIe siècles," *Atti del congresso internazionale di scienze storiche* IX (Rome, 1904): 147–69, and "Des renunciations au moyen âge et dans notre ancien droit," *Nouvelle revue de droit français et étranger* 24 (1900): 108–42 and 25 (1901): 241–77. On medieval coinage, see Peter Spufford, *Handbook of Medieval Exchange* (London: Offices of the Royal Historical Society, University College London, 1986).

The legal history background of southern France has been masterfully recreated by André Gouron, "Diffusion des consulats méridionaux et expansion du droit romain aux XIIe et XIIIe siècles," *Bibliothèque de l'Ecole des Chartes* 121 (1963): 26–76; "Enseignement du droit, légistes et canonistes dans le Midi de la France à la fin du XIIIe et au début du XIVe siècle," *Recueil de mémoires et travaux publié par la société d'histoire du droit et des institutions des anciens pays de droit écrit*, fasc. V (Montpellier, 1966), 1–33; "Les étapes de la pénétration du droit romain en Septimanie," *Annales du Midi* 69 (1957): 103–20; *La réglementation des métiers en Languedoc au moyen âge* (Geneva, Paris, 1958); "Le rôle social des juristes dans les villes méridionales au moyen-âge," *Villes de l'Europe méditerranéenne et de l'Europe occidentale du moyen-âge au XIXe siècle. Annales de la Faculté des Lettres et Sciences Humaines de Nice*, nos. 9–10 (1969), 55–67; and, with Jean Hilaire, "Les «sceaux» rigoureux du Midi de la France," *Recueil de mémoires et travaux publié par la société d'histoire du droit et des institutions des anciens pays de droit écrit*, fasc. IV, 1 (1958), 41–77. See also Jean Hilaire, "Pratique notariale et influence universitaire à Montpellier à la fin du moyen âge," *Hommage à André Dupont. Etudes médiévales languedociennes*, Fédération Historique du Languedoc méditerranéen et du Roussillon (Montpellier: Université Paul-Valéry, 1974), 167–78.

INDEX

Medieval Institute Publications is a program
of The Medieval Institute, College of
Arts and Sciences, Western Michigan
University.

Typeset in 10/13 Caslon
Designed by Linda K. Judy
Composed by Julie Scrivener
at Medieval Institute Publications
Manufactured by Cushing-Malloy, Inc.—Ann Arbor, Michigan

Medieval Institute Publications
College of Arts and Sciences
Western Michigan University
1903 W. Michigan Ave.
Kalamazoo, MI 49008-5432
www.wmich.edu/medieval

 WESTERN MICHIGAN UNIVERSITY